You Gotta Have

G.U.T.S.

How Gratitude, Unity, Trustworthiness, and Spirituality Empowered a Sharecropper's Daughter to Conquer the American Dream.

Martha Daniel

Assessing Your G.U.T.S.

*D*reaming big requires courage and determination, but most importantly, it requires alignment with the principles of Gratitude, Unity, Trustworthiness, and Spirituality. This exercise will help you assess your own G.U.T.S. and inspire you to take actionable steps toward achieving your dreams.

Visit **MarthaDaniel.com** and download the exercise.

Praises for Martha Daniel and G.U.T.S.

Martha and I met at a women's conference (in the ladies' room) over two decades ago. My journey with Martha started as a business alliance. We bonded and decided we would forever be in each other's lives. Her leadership, guidance, and beliefs are everything I aspire to. Martha is an inspiration and a role model for the ages. I am forever grateful for her G.U.T.S.

Deborah Larrison
Senior C-level financial industry executive

It has been an honor to know Martha Daniel for more than twenty-five years. Her depth of caring for humanity is a testament to her philanthropic heart. As a philanthropist, Martha's tenacity, intelligence, and vision have led her to great success. Her personal integrity, warmth, and fearlessness make it a true pleasure to work with her.

Sue Parks
President and CEO, Orange County United Way

While starting and growing a business is not for the faint of heart, Martha has grown her business with a team of loyal and hardworking people. Through all the ups and downs of business ownership, Martha has shown persistence and has never shied away from giving back to her community, church, friends, and family.

Irene Kinoshita
Retired entrepreneur

Professionally, I have admired Martha for many years, not only as a remarkable woman of color in technology, but also as a trailblazing entrepreneur whose journey I find deeply inspiring. Martha meets every obstacle with grace, courage, and unwavering resilience. Watching her lead, and seeing the way she uplifts those around her, has shaped my own understanding of what true leadership and championing others looks like. Time and again she has demonstrated the power of faith, perseverance, and hope. She has given me the confidence to stand boldly on my purpose and to never underestimate the strength it takes to have G.U.T.S. when facing life's biggest challenges.

Doniel Sutton
Chief People Officer, Pinterest

Martha is one of the most remarkable individuals I have ever known. She has a unique blend of creativity, intelligence, and empathy. Over the years, I have witnessed her incredible work ethic and passion for her business. Her dedication to her business and her unwavering commitment to excellence have been a constant source of inspiration for everyone who has had the pleasure of working with her. Martha is not only a talented professional, but she is also a person of exceptional character.

Sandra Floyd
Founder, President/CEO @ OUTSOURCE Consulting Services, Inc.

Martha has boundless energy to devote to her business, family, friends, church, and veteran organizations. She is a delight to work with, and I have always enjoyed learning from her.

Hoshi Printer
Independent Director

Beyond her professional achievements, Martha is deeply grounded in family and faith. She epitomizes compassion, resilience, and optimism. Her life is a model of resilience, generosity, and integrity.

Betty Lamar
Retired IT/Nonprofit Executive

Rev. Martha Daniel is an international leader and woman for all seasons. She inspired me and so many to come out of personal inhibitions, fear, and self-destructive behaviors. Her leadership helped build a church with no property, to own property all over America. She is an awesome preacher, community leader, and lover of God's kingdom.

Rev. Dr. Mark Whitlock
Pastor Reid Temple AME Church

Martha is an exceptionally intelligent and accomplished entrepreneur whose skills and vision are truly inspiring. I have always admired her loving relationship with her children and husband, a reflection of her values and strength. She has a remarkable ability to inspire and uplift those around her, making her not only a cherished friend, but also a truly extraordinary individual.

Ruth Ko
Publisher Emeritus Orange Coast Magazine
Artist, Actress

To my husband, Daniel, whose unwavering support and
encouragement gave me the strength to pause and share
my story in hopes of inspiring others.

For my children, their children, and all future generations.
May this work serve as a beacon of inspiration and a reminder
of the power of tenacity and belief in oneself.

To all those who dare to dream and pursue their aspirations
with G.U.T.S.
I salute your resilience and courage.

Table of Contents

What Is G.U.T.S.?

G.U.T.S. is more than an acronym, it's a way of life built on gratitude, unity, trustworthiness, and spirituality.

Dreams are powerful, are they not? They nudge us, inspire us, and won't let go until we pay attention. But let's be honest: turning dreams into reality can feel like climbing a mountain. Fear, uncertainty, financial sacrifices, or the fear of failing are enough to make anyone hesitate. Sound familiar? You are not alone.

Welcome to the world of G.U.T.S.—Gratitude, Unity, Trustworthiness, and Spirituality. These are the tools you can use to tackle challenges and turn your dreams into reality, one step at a time.

My life has been all about pushing through the lows that have come my way, and believe me, I have encountered them at every turn. From segregation and discrimination in 1960s Memphis, Tennessee, to an unplanned teenage pregnancy, a less-than-ideal marriage, business partners who stole from me, personal bankruptcy, and even the heartbreak of losing a child to suicide —those lows made me question everything in life.

Through it all, my faith, my dreams, and my integrity, coupled with my G.U.T.S., kept me going. These core values helped me survive and thrive.

Despite all those lows, God built in some critical highs to encourage me to keep going. From earning my way into workplaces that valued my input, to starting successful companies, winning multi-million-dollar contracts, and meeting the love of my life, the highs have certainly outweighed the lows. Those highs gave me hope and reminded me of what was possible. Even though I had moments of hopelessness, I learned that persistence, faith, and not giving up are key, even when everything feels uncertain. The ups and downs, the good and the bad, bring lessons. Sure, life can be stressful at times, but I learned that every experience moved me closer to my dream. I didn't give up, I kept going, and it was worth it. I experienced a beautiful rainbow at the end of the storm.

As a trailblazing entrepreneur and CEO of two high-profile companies in the technology field, I have been through it all, and I can tell you this: Success does not happen by accident. It takes clarity, determination, and a solid strategy. Success in any pursuit is possible, and it starts with dreaming big, making a plan, staying confident, and working hard. From there, you have to activate the power that resides deep inside you.

That is where G.U.T.S. comes in. In this book, I break success down into simple, actionable steps you can follow. You'll learn how to face fear head-on, build unshakable confidence, say goodbye to "no" as the final answer, and prepare for the sacrifices needed to make your dream a reality. You'll discover the importance of practicing Gratitude, Unity, Trustworthiness, and Spirituality, qualities that have kept me grounded through life's toughest moments.

I am a big dreamer who does not back down from challenges, and I owe it all to G.U.T.S. These four principles have been my guide, helping me achieve success beyond what I imagined.

G – Gratitude

Gratitude is essential in your journey toward success. It is the cornerstone that reminds you to appreciate every small victory and allows you to recognize the generous support you receive along the way. Practicing gratitude builds a positive mindset and deepens your commitment to your goals.

Along my journey, gratitude was that silent, positive voice reminding me to value each accomplishment and every step I took, whether good or challenging, as a milestone toward my dream. Whenever I led with gratitude, I found peace of mind and renewed strength to keep going.

Gratitude is a humble reminder that your accomplishments are not solitary, but a beautiful blending of hard work, determination, and help from others. Every achievement reflects not just my effort, but also the generosity, guidance, and encouragement of others. Learning to say thank you without pride helped me maintain a humble spirit and made it easy for people to help when I needed advice or assistance. Gratitude opened many doors for me because people appreciated the simple acts of gratitude I expressed.

Gratitude gives you the right attitude to seize success when it becomes available. Therefore, do not lack gratitude as you journey toward your dreams. When you cultivate an attitude of gratitude, you invite new opportunities and keep yourself aligned with what truly matters. Gratitude enriches your journey, strengthens your character, and prepares you to recognize and seize success when it arrives.

U – Unity

Unity also reminds us that success is never a solo pursuit. The relationships you build along your journey are among your greatest assets. Surrounding yourself with people who share your vision and values gives you strength, inspiration, and support when things get tough. It is easy to fall into the trap of thinking you have to do everything on your own, but lasting success grows through connection and collaboration.

I've achieved what I have because I wasn't afraid to ask for help. My network played a huge role in helping me reach my goals. So many people contributed to my journey: friends, family, neighbors, church members, mentors, customers, advocates, veterans, my husband . . . the list goes on. My success didn't happen in a vacuum, and yours won't either. When you embrace unity, you find strength in numbers. Your network will encourage you, lift you up, and help you turn your dreams into reality.

Unity connects you to a world of opportunities and possibilities. One string on its own can't make a strong rope. You need others—their strength, wisdom, and encouragement—to help you reach your dreams. You will always need someone to help you, whether to listen to your ideas, give feedback, or answer your questions. Your dreams are never just about you; they always have an impact on others. They are a shared symbol of hope, effort, and resilience.

T – Trustworthiness

Reaching your goals is not about ticking boxes. It's about *how* you achieve them. Trustworthiness is built on integrity, honesty, and reliability, characteristics that can shape your reputation and the relationships you build. When people know they can depend on you, they respect you, support you, and want to work with you. Trustworthiness should be at the foundation of who you are.

Honesty and integrity aren't extras, they're essential. Trust takes time to build, but it can be broken in an instant and can take a lifetime to rebuild. That is why your reputation matters so much.

Integrity guides everything I do. I've had plenty of chances to take shortcuts that might have sped up my financial success, but they never sat right with me. Staying true to what's right and holding onto my values mattered more than quick rewards. There were moments when doing the right thing was difficult, but the peace of mind and respect I gained in return were worth far more. I wouldn't trade the trust and respect I have built for anything. It has always been about doing what's right.

S – Spirituality

Spirituality connects you to God and to a purpose greater than yourself. It provides the inner strength and resilience to keep going even when things feel uncertain. Faith becomes an inner compass, guiding your steps, calming your fears, and allowing you to believe in something bigger than yourself and to trust the journey when the road gets tough. It can transform the way you approach your goals and help you navigate those moments when the answers aren't clear and no one else can help. It is in those times that God steps in.

Ever since I was a young girl, I've been active in my faith. I began singing in church at five and teaching Sunday school at ten. My mother always told me that I had a special calling from God, and though I didn't see it then, I came to understand what she meant. As an ordained minister and Bible study teacher, I've seen how staying spiritually grounded supports both personal growth and professional success.

In moments of weakness, God's strength has been my anchor. He has always given me what I needed to push through obstacles and keep going. Over time, I have realized that I cannot accomplish my dreams or goals without Him because I am limited in my wisdom, even when smart in knowledge. Once I learned that I gain my wisdom from God, my successes multiplied. As I worked toward my dreams, my faith grew stronger. I started to see every challenge as an opportunity to grow spiritually, personally, and professionally.

As an entrepreneur, my journey has had its share of trials, but my faith has always carried me through. I held onto my faith, trusting that God would see me through, just as He promised. When challenges came, my connection to Him kept me grounded. Looking back, I know that faith was the foundation that got me through it all.

G.U.T.S. is more than an acronym. It's a way of life built on gratitude, unity, trustworthiness, and spirituality. If you've put your dreams on the back burner, it's time to turn up the heat and position yourself for success. G.U.T.S. is about perseverance, staying focused, and finding clarity on what you want. Picture yourself as a relentless dreamer, steady and unshakable. Now, ask yourself: *How far am I willing to go to turn my dream into reality? How can I activate my G.U.T.S. to achieve my dream?*

Success is closer than you think. It starts with centering your values around G.U.T.S. Let's get started.

I Got It From My Mama

*Success comes to those who hold gratitude close, unify their
efforts with those around them, build their dreams on trust,
and keep their faith strong. It's not about waiting for the
threads of fate to weave themselves; it's about grabbing hold
of them, unravelling their mysteries, and creating something
extraordinary.*

My Mama was four feet, ten inches short and a little stocky with a heavy chest, but when she was in the room, you knew she was in charge. She didn't need to raise her voice; her words carried weight on their own. She was stern but polite, and you never had to guess what she meant. She made herself clear.

Mama didn't have much formal education, but you would never know it. She worked hard to speak proper English and always avoided broken grammar. She used to say she never wanted anyone to figure out if she was educated or not, and it was not their business. Mama had style, too. She was classy, sharp as a tack, and could dress to impress. As a seamstress, she could whip up anything, with or without a pattern. She had a natural grace, and the community loved her for it. People admired her for her honesty and integrity, and it was obvious that she was a woman who loved God.

When I think about the life I have built—rooted in tenacity, faith, and determination—it's clear that my story is deeply tied to my Mama's. Even though we grew up in different times and faced our own unique challenges, there is a thread of resilience that connects us. From Mama, I inherited the drive to push past the boundaries created by the segregation we were both born into. Her courage, wisdom, and philosophy are woven into my own journey, like threads in a beautiful tapestry.

Mama was born in 1925 in Como, Mississippi, the eldest of six children in a sharecropping family. Segregation, racism, and fear were part of daily life under Jim Crow laws. Opportunities were scarce for Mama's family, which meant working the cotton fields in exchange for a place to live, and having just enough money to scrape by.

Sharecropping began after the Civil War ended slavery and upended the South's plantation labor system. Landowners needed workers for their fields, so they offered formerly enslaved people an arrangement that sounded like a fair deal on the surface: a place to stay, small payments throughout the year, and a share of the crop. But in reality, it was a trap. Every year after the harvest, landowners would "reconcile" the accounts. Most sharecroppers, like Mama's family, didn't have the education to understand the numbers, and somehow, they always ended up in debt. It was a system designed to keep them stuck, never able to gain independence.

Mama's father eventually had enough of it. He left Mississippi for Arkansas, hoping to find a better job, but that meant leaving the family behind. With her mother often sick, Mama, as the eldest, had to step up and work in the fields to help keep things going.

I never got to meet my grandmother. Mama told me she passed away at only thirty-three. Losing her mom shattered Mama's world. And if that wasn't hard enough, her father came back for the funeral, but instead of staying, he took Mama's siblings with him to Arkansas and left Mama behind. She was only sixteen. Can you imagine? Sixteen and left to fend for herself. Mama's story is one of resilience. It is a reminder of how hard life was for so many back then.

When Mama told me this story, she cried like the pain was still fresh.

"My daddy never liked me. I don't know why," she said. "After Mama died, he came to the house and took my three sisters and brother with him to Arkansas."

She paused for a moment, then added, "When I ran after them, begging to go too, he yelled at me to go back to the house. He said he wasn't taking me."

Mama looked down, her words heavy. "When I kept running after him, he pushed me to the ground and told me to get back. He said I wasn't going."

Even though twenty years had passed, I could see how much it still hurt her to remember that moment. She told me one of the neighbors saw what happened and ran down the road and picked her up, taking her back to their house. Mama said she didn't see her father again until she was twenty-five, and after that visit, she never saw him again.

"I'll never know why he never liked me," she said, shaking her head, her shoulders hunched, "but I know he did not treat me like he treated my siblings. He was really mean to me."

All that loss could have been enough to break anyone, but not Mama. Instead, it fueled her to stand on her own two feet and keep going, no matter how tough life got. Eventually, she went to live with her Uncle Jake and Aunt Agnes in Memphis. For the first time, she got the chance to go to school, but it wasn't easy. At sixteen, she sat in classrooms full of much younger kids. Eventually, the teasing and embarrassment became too much, so she quit school and got married, trying to create a way out of the life she'd been dealt. Marriage, though, brought its own struggles. Mama's first marriage was to the father of my older brother, Ray. It didn't last. Her husband wanted to take her back to Mississippi, and she refused to return to the life she had worked so hard to leave behind. Determined to build a new life in Memphis, Mama made the tough choice to end the marriage.

A few years later, she married Charlie White, with whom she had Vance and Charlett, my other two siblings. But that marriage wasn't a walk in the park either.

"Charlie was a pretty boy and lazy. He didn't want to work," Mama always said.

While Mama's oldest son Ray lived nearby with her Aunt Agnes in Whitehaven, Tennessee, Mama worked two jobs to make ends meet for herself and her other two children. Mama balanced two waitressing jobs to support the family, eventually realizing her limits and making another tough decision to end her second marriage. She left Charlie and temporarily moved back in with Aunt Agnes and Uncle Jake.

Even with all the challenges she faced, Mama never let herself get discouraged. She kept pushing and relying on her determination to build a better life. Despite it all, working two jobs and being a single parent even though she was married, she kept moving forward.

Mama's third marriage was to Reverend John Warren Stiggers, my biological father. He was much older than Mama and a preacher at the local church. Unfortunately, that relationship was full of physical abuse, and once again, Mama had the courage to walk away. Not long after she left him, Reverend Stiggers passed away. I was only two years old at the time.

No matter how hard life got, Mama's dedication to building a better life for herself and her family never wavered. She was determined to keep a roof over our heads, no matter how hard she had to work. She put in long hours but never lost sight of being a good mom. Making sure we had a safe home and access to education was her purpose in life. She never faltered when it came to providing for her family. She would sew our clothes by hand, stretch meals to feed us all, and juggle multiple jobs to make sure we were taken care of. She had an incredible spirit that would not break.

Some evenings I'd sit with her while she sewed, and she would share all kinds of stories with me. One time, she told me how, as a child, she could look up through the roof at night and see the stars.

"And in the morning," she said with a chuckle, "the sunlight streaming in was our alarm clock."

She'd laugh, reminiscing about how the rooster ruled over the chickens she could see through the gaps in the wood plank floor. The house was a typical two-room structure, unpainted with a tin roof and resting on a few pillars.

"That rooster," she'd say, "he pecked at them and scared them half to death, acting like he was king of the world."

Then she'd look at me and say, "Baby, you don't know nothing about that kind of hard life. No baby, you don't know about getting up before dawn, going to the fields, planting and weeding the harvest, working from sunrise to sunset."

Mama shook her head as she reflected on her childhood.

"Your dress was made from the potato sacks, and it cut your skin every time you moved, and you worked the fields with no shoes at all, barefoot. The little joy of laughter we had was looking through the holes in the floor before bedtime watching the rooster control the chickens."

She looked at me.

"As long as I am alive, you will never live like that."

Every time she said that I felt a deep sense of safety, like no matter what, Mama had me. I knew she meant every word.

Mama told me how she'd see other children heading to the one-room schoolhouse for Black children as she worked in the fields picking cotton.

"I wanted so badly to go to school, even for a few days," she said one time, wiping her eyes. "But Mama told me I couldn't. We wouldn't have food to eat or a place to sleep if I didn't work in the fields. My daddy had left us, and somebody had to keep us going."

Even as she dried her tears, I could feel the weight of a pain that still hurt, even after all those years. But Mama never let go of her dream of getting an education. She chipped away at it, little by little, over the years. At thirty-six, she started night school. And at seventy-two, she finally got her GED.

"It's never too late to live your dreams," she'd say, and she lived by those words.

Watching her achieve that goal taught me that persistence and faith can overcome anything. Mama gave us more than a home—she gave us purpose and hope for a better future. Her life is proof that even in the hardest times, hard work and determination can lead to brighter days. She never let go of her belief that faith and effort would create something better, for herself and for all of us. That belief shines through in the legacy she left behind.

I became the first in the family to earn a college degree, paving the way for my brother, the late Rev. Jerome Scales, and the rest of my siblings. Jerome and I went on to earn master's degrees, and the other three pursued successful school careers. All of us fulfilled Mama's dream of making sure our family would not lack education.

Her unwavering determination changed the trajectory of our family, and her legacy continues to inspire us all, living on through three generations of highly accomplished children and grandchildren who have succeeded as university professors, teachers, and school principals. There is an employment labor law attorney, a vice president at a financial institution, a tech company president, pastors, preachers, engineers, an executive social worker, and a human resources manager. And now, a generation of great-grandchildren is stepping up, pursuing degrees in music, business, theology, psychology, international studies, and kinesiology. It's amazing to see how far we have come—all thanks to my Mama, a sharecropper's daughter from Como, Mississippi.

Mama's strong qualities—her G.U.T.S.—were the foundation of her incredible story. Her life is proof that one person's courage and strength can ripple through generations, inspiring dreamers like me to keep pushing forward. Through it all, Mama never lost her compassion. She survived life's chaos and rose above it, creating a home filled with love and stability for her family. She didn't teach us by lecturing or forcing her beliefs on us. She taught us by living them every day.

Even when life became unbearably hard, Mama's faith never wavered. She was a loyal believer, and we went to church all day on Sundays so that Mama could instill in us the same faith that had brought her through countless life challenges. Many nights, I'd peep into Mama's room and see her on her knees praying. She believed in something bigger than herself, and that belief kept her going. It inspired everyone around her to keep pushing forward too. Mama's life taught us that real strength does not come from avoiding struggles, it comes from facing them head-on, never giving up, and working toward a better future.

One of Mama's favorite things to say to me was, "Martha, there are street signs named after you: 'One Way.'" She'd pull that out whenever she thought I was being especially stubborn.

On one occasion, I sat with Mama in her living room, feeling a little nervous to tell her I was planning to join the Navy.

"Mama, I need to leave Memphis," I said. "I'm really unhappy with my marriage, my career, and my future. So, I've decided to join the Navy, and I'll be leaving in two months."

Mama didn't miss a beat.

"What do you mean?" she shot back. "You've got a brand-new house, a husband with a great job, and you are doing fine at work. You are going to leave all that and join the military? Have you lost your mind? How can you be unhappy when you have everything going for you? And the military? That's no place for a woman!"

I looked at her and said, "Mama, none of those things matter. I'm not happy, and I haven't been able to achieve the goals I set for myself."

She stood up, put her hands on her hips, and gave me one of her classic looks. "What more could you possibly want in life that you don't already have?" As I opened my mouth to explain, she cut me off.

"You only think about yourself. Life for you is one way—they even make street signs about you: 'One Way!'" Then, as she stormed toward her bedroom, she yelled back, "You only care about doing things your way, no matter what anyone else thinks! You are so stubborn. The military is no place for you, and what about your husband and your child? You need to think about that, Ms. One Way."

She slammed her bedroom door, leaving me sitting there on the sofa, questioning everything. But I had already made up my mind, and even if Mama didn't agree, I was going to do it. She'd called me "One Way" plenty of times before, but this time was different. I could tell she was not just calling me stubborn; she was worried.

I understood her reaction. She only wanted the best for me. She thought I had more than she ever did, and she couldn't wrap her head around why I was unhappy or willing to give it all up. But Mama also knew me well enough to know that once I made up my mind, there was no changing it.

The funny thing is, I got that "one way" attitude from her. When she decided on something, that was it; Mama would make it happen, no matter what. She worked hard, controlled what she could, and didn't let anyone stand in her way when it came to what she believed was best for her and her family. I guess I am more like her than she realized.

Mama always taught me to never give up, no matter how hard things got. She lived that lesson every day, especially in the way she continued to educate herself. She had self-learning books on all kinds of topics, and she'd study them constantly. She even had a book that helped her practice writing properly, and sometimes she'd ask me to help her with pronunciation.

Throughout my childhood, Mama was always taking some kind of class or home course, always learning something new. She was determined to "speak educated," as she called it, and she believed in always improving yourself. She taught my siblings and me that reading and writing were privileges, not things to take for granted. She reminded us that she was deprived of a proper education, and because of that, her job options were limited.

She worked as a maid in the executive office of a manufacturing company that made dinette sets, but she hated being called by that title. To her, a maid was a job for the uneducated, and she wanted better for us. She constantly pushed us to take school seriously. And if a teacher ever called Mama about one of her children not doing their schoolwork, we were in big trouble! She had an incredible determination to make sure we had opportunities of which she could only dream. Even after long, exhausting days at work, she would find the energy to help with school projects, show up at our events, and push us to aim higher.

She always told us that with prayer, hard work, and perseverance, we could do anything. Even when we doubted ourselves, she believed in us completely. That belief became the spark that kept me going and reaching for more. Looking back, I realize how much she sacrificed for us. She poured so much of her life into building a strong, supportive foundation for her family. Whether it was her dedication to learning, her strong work ethic, her commitment to church, or her creativity as a seamstress and milliner, she showed me what it means to give your all. As a mother, wife, and so much more, Mama's love shaped me, molded me into someone stronger and better. It's a legacy I carry with me every day, and I try to honor it in everything I do. This legacy is G.U.T.S.

A Story of Unity: From Mr. Scales to "Daddy"

One of my favorite stories that demonstrates the power of unity is how Mr. Sammie Scales became my daddy. It all started when Mama introduced us to Mr. Scales. She mentioned he worked with her, and at first, he was just a friendly visitor. But after a few visits, I noticed something special about him, a kindness, a warmth, and a sense of companionship. I didn't want him to be a visitor anymore. I wanted him to be my daddy.

Months went by and Mr. Scales came around more often, bringing so much joy and playfulness into our home. One day, I couldn't help myself, and I asked him, "Can I call you Daddy?"

He smiled at me, and with the kindest voice, he said, "Absolutely, you can call me Daddy."

Excited, I ran into the kitchen to tell Mama the good news, but her reaction was not what I expected. Mama grabbed me by my hand and walked to the living room where Mr. Scales was sitting on the sofa.

"She cannot call you Daddy," she firmly told Mr. Scales. My heart sank, and tears filled my eyes.

But then after Mama left the room, Mr. Scales said something that changed everything. He looked at me and said, "Soon, you'll call me Daddy because I am going to marry your mama."

I didn't really understand what marriage meant back then. I also didn't fully grasp the absence of my birth father. All I knew was that soon after Christmas, I could call Mr. Scales Daddy, and that made me so happy. True to his words, he married Mama on January 9, 1957, two days after my birthday. And just like that, Mr. Scales was not a visitor anymore. He was my daddy!

Looking back, I sometimes wonder if he would have decided to marry Mama if it hadn't been for the bond he and I shared. I never held back from letting him know how much I wanted him to be my daddy, and I think my persistence played a big part in his decision to become my father. Daddy wanted a family, and I think he loved being called Daddy. And Mama? She had so much to offer him too. She was beautiful, with a dynamic personality. Together, they built a home full of love, support, and respect.

Back then, Daddy had no idea he had a son named Jerome. One day, a friend called to tell him that Jerome's mother, Betty, had left for New York and that Jerome, about five years old, had been left behind. Daddy didn't know any of this because he'd been incarcerated for around five years, and Betty never told him.

Jerome was staying with one of Betty's relatives in North Memphis, but Daddy's friend said they weren't treating him right. Next thing I knew, Jerome showed up at our house. And just like that, there were four of us kids under one roof—Charlett, Vance, me, and now Daddy's son, Jerome.

Not long after Daddy married Mama, we were all sitting at the dinner table eating when Daddy looked around at us and said, "This is how this family is going to work. I am your Daddy." Then he looked over at Mama and added, "That's your Mama, and that's what you'll call us."

He kept eating for a moment, then looked back up and said, "All of y'all are brothers and sisters. I don't want to hear anyone saying, 'Step Daddy,' 'Step Mama,' or 'Step anything.' We don't use that word in this house. I am your Daddy, she's your Mama, and y'all are brothers and sisters. Got it?"

I looked up at him and said, "You are my Daddy."

He smiled and said, "That's right, baby. I am your Daddy."

He and Mama never had children together, but from the start, Daddy was clear about his role and wanted us to feel like a real family. He and Mama had two different parenting styles. Mama was all about discipline and getting things done, no excuses. Daddy was the opposite; he wanted me to think things through, speak my mind, and learn how to soften my approach when needed. While Mama told me to stay in my place, Daddy encouraged my curiosity and self-expression. Their styles clashed sometimes, but together, they helped shape who I am.

Mama would give me instructions, and I would immediately ask, "Why?" It drove her nuts, and sometimes she would shut down my questions. Daddy, on the other hand, loved my questions. He even gave me tips on how to stand my ground without being too harsh.

"You are going to be somebody big one day," he told me once. At the time, I didn't really get it, but that simple statement stuck with me and made me believe I could do something great.

Because I liked to ask questions and understand the "whys" behind things, it usually got me into trouble with Mama. She saw my curiosity as being disrespectful or argumentative, which led to more than a few whippings. When I raised my children, though, I realized how important it is to let them express their thoughts, even if I didn't agree. At the very least, I wanted them to feel heard. I think I got that from my Daddy. Even when he didn't agree with what I was saying or how I was acting, he always let me talk. Then, instead of scolding me, he'd ask questions that helped me figure things out on my own. Looking back, I realize both Mama and Daddy taught me valuable lessons in their own ways.

Once, when I was in the sixth grade, I brought home my report card, all excited to show my parents my straight-A marks. When Mama saw I also had all "U's" for unsatisfactory conduct, she started yelling. "What are you doing at school to get all these U's? Why are you behaving like this?" She kept reading and saw notes about me talking too much and being too aggressive, which only made her angrier.

Daddy, on the other hand, approached it differently. He asked me to sit down so we could talk. He started by praising me.

"I like that you are smart. Bringing home all A's is really good."

I smiled and even blushed a bit. His approval meant the world to me. Then, he looked me in the eyes, and I knew something serious was coming.

"You are very smart," he said, "but I want you to learn one thing in life: Nobody likes an educated fool."

I was crushed. Those words hit me harder than any punishment Mama could've given. I started crying because the thought of Daddy thinking I was a fool was devastating. From that point on, I made it a priority to manage my behavior in class, showing respect yet being firm when necessary, and avoiding being loud or drawing negative attention without reason.

Daddy's words had a lasting impact. He never raised his hand to discipline me, but his words had so much power that they brought about instant change. That moment shaped how I approached everything. Daddy taught me that words matter. When used thoughtfully and without anger, they can bring better results than any argument or punishment.

Mama's drive and strength combined with Daddy's strategy and patience have helped me grow, tackle challenges, and reach my goals. Mama set the tone for discipline and resilience, while Daddy's thoughtful guidance helped me figure out how to approach the world with purpose. Together, their lessons created a balance—a mix of strength and curiosity, grit and grace. That balance has been a big part of who I am, and it shows up in my conversations with my husband, children, grandchildren, managers, employees, and friends. Growing up in such a dynamic environment taught me a lot about adaptability.

Daddy had a quiet way of showing me how powerful self-expression can be. He always encouraged me to explore my ideas and speak my mind, even if my thoughts were a little unconventional. Whenever I talked to him about school and told him how I excelled at something, he'd light up and say, "Baby, Daddy is so proud of you. Keep up the good work because you are going places."

Hearing those words always made me smile. I could feel how proud he was, and that encouragement gave me the confidence to believe in myself.

When I graduated from junior college in Memphis and started applying for jobs, I hit a lot of roadblocks. Those rejections were tough, and I would go to Daddy feeling disappointed, knowing I should have gotten the job. He would always reassure me.

"It's gonna happen for you," he would say. "Don't let them make you feel like you are not smart, because you really are. Sometimes they overlook you because you are a Negro, but you gonna be alright."

The way he said it was so convincing, it gave me hope that things would get better.

From my parents, I learned that success is not about talent or ambition, it's about perseverance, staying true to your values, and adapting to whatever life throws at you. When Mama looked at me as a kid and said, "You could be somebody big," she was not talking to me in that moment, she was talking to my future and to the generations that would come after me that might one day doubt their ability to keep going.

As the CEO of two growing tech companies, I owe so much of my success to the values Mama taught me. My mother's teachings inspired my G.U.T.S. philosophy. She lived it every single day. Her story proves that even the humblest beginnings can lead to something extraordinary. Whether I am mentoring young professionals, speaking at community events, or leading my companies, I always make it a point to share G.U.T.S. and the values behind it. These are not lessons that work for only certain people, they are universal.

As I pass that torch forward, I am filled with gratitude for the woman who had the G.U.T.S. to turn her struggles into something beautiful, for herself and for all of us. The torch she lit in me now burns throughout every generation of our family. When I read the University of Chicago Law School application essay my daughter Maronya wrote, I could see my mama's spirit in every word. Maronya shared a story about her grandmother taking her to visit the cotton fields she had worked in as a young girl. In the essay, Maronya wrote that she could not wait to graduate with her law degree and go to stand there with her grandmother and say, "Grandmama, look how far we have come from these cotton fields in Mississippi."

One of the biggest realizations I have had is that Mama's influence goes far beyond our family. Her lessons in G.U.T.S. touch the lives of everyone I meet and work with. I have learned to lead with gratitude, build unity in teams, stay trustworthy no matter what, and rely on my spirituality for strength and clarity. These values are my compass, guiding me in everything I do. I have seen teams come together through unity and trust, people lifted up by gratitude, and obstacles overcome with spirituality. Every time I experience these moments, I am reminded of the incredible ripple effect one life can have when it's lived with purpose and intention.

Mama's legacy belongs to everyone who hears it through my actions, my leadership, and my story. By honoring the wisdom she passed down to me, I helped others discover their own strength, define their own values, and make their own impact. Her legacy continues to guide me, and my G.U.T.S. philosophy is my way of sharing her wisdom with the world.

Lessons in G.U.T.S.

G — Gratitude: Mama always found something to be thankful for, no matter how tough things got. She had a way of seeing the good in the smallest things. She appreciated the simple things: a roof over our heads, food on the table, and the warmth of family around her. These were blessings she worked for tirelessly, often sacrificing her own needs to make sure we were taken care of. Her gratitude was a quiet but constant reminder of what really mattered in life.

U — Unity: She held our family together, always putting us first no matter what the circumstances. She provided for our needs, and she created a home filled with love, laughter, and understanding. She reminded us to be there for each other, through the highs and lows, teaching us the value of unity and compassion. Her countless sacrifices, often unspoken, kept us strong and connected, showing us the true meaning of family.

T — Trustworthiness: Mama's words were gold. When she made a promise, everyone knew she would keep it. People respected her because she always came through, whether it was at work, (where she was known for her reliability and dedication), at home (where her family leaned on her strength and wisdom), or in her relationships (where she offered unwavering loyalty and support).

You could always count on Mama to do what she said, regardless of the challenge.

S — Spirituality: Her unwavering faith in God gave her the strength to face even the hardest days, providing a source of comfort and resilience when challenges seemed insurmountable. It was her anchor, keeping her grounded and steady when life felt overwhelming, reminding her that she was never alone, no matter how heavy the burden. Through prayer and trust, she found the courage to keep moving forward, drawing peace from her belief that everything had a purpose.

CHAPTER 3

Dealing with Unfairness and Bias

*You cannot defeat discrimination or segregation by standing
on the outside. Fighting fire with fire only creates more flames.
Real change happens when you step into the system and work
to change it from within.*

Segregation was my daily reality growing up in Memphis. The signs were everywhere. "Colored Only" or "No Colored Allowed" signs were plastered on everything from filthy public restrooms to the back doors of doctor's offices. The "Whites Only" water fountains were clean and shiny, while those for Black people were rusted and falling apart.

Growing up under the burden of segregation that allowed discrimination in practically every area of life shaped how I see the world as an adult, how I approach leadership, and how I tackle change. Many people who lived through segregation emerged with a bitterness sharp enough to cut through a block of ice. But not me. I survived segregation with the will and determination to navigate a world full of injustice and fight back with patience, intelligence, and humanity. Thanks to some amazing mentors and life lessons, I learned to push back against a broken system without letting anger take over, and I gained a resilience that has helped me overcome some of life's most difficult experiences.

But my mama? She was a force of nature. Her strength and determination still blow me away. She made sure my siblings and I avoided the dirty water fountains or the rundown restrooms. She even carried a little tin cup so we didn't have to touch the dirty fountain. Her actions were a quiet rebellion, small but powerful ways to hold onto our dignity even when the system was stacked against us. Mama's optimism kept us going, even when the injustices we faced felt like too much to bear.

Not long after we moved to a new neighborhood, Mama and I went to a doctor's office. We drove up to the entrance, got out of the car, and walked up to the front door. When we stepped inside, the waiting room was full of White people who immediately turned and stared at us.

The lady behind the desk stood up and said, "You know the Colored entrance is in the back."

Mama grabbed my hand, smiled politely, and said, "I am sorry, we are new here. I did not realize. Thank you."

But I was not having it. I said loudly, "Mama, where are we going? I thought we were going to the doctor here."

She leaned down and said softly, "We are, baby. We just have to go to another part of the office." Then she quietly led me outside, around to the back door. That's when I saw the sign: "Colored Only Entrance."

I was frustrated and confused. "Mama," I asked, "why do we have to go here? I can still see the other people in the front room."

She didn't answer right away. She squeezed my hand, walked us to the few chairs in the "Colored Waiting Room," and whispered, "Baby, Dr. King is working on this. Things are going to change." Then, like always, she smiled calmly and added, "When Dr. King fixes things, you are going to be ready. You need to stay in school, get your education, and be ready for better days."

Mama had a way of taking even the most humiliating situations and turning them into lessons about hope and perseverance. She really believed change was coming, and she made sure we were ready for it. Her faith in education and preparation became my foundation. It fueled my ambition and my quiet resistance.

Even though we didn't have much money, my parents worked long hours, two and three jobs. Though it was hard, they saved up to buy a new home in 1959, in Holiday Heights. We were so excited to move into our new three-bedroom house made of brick and stone, with a huge backyard where we could run around and play. It was a neighborhood where White families still lived, but for Black children like us, opportunities were far from equal. Schools were still segregated. The White families were moving out, and eventually it became an all-Black neighborhood. On our street there were so many children that it really felt like one big family. All the neighbors looked out for each other, and every mom had the authority to keep the children in line. If you got out of hand, you could expect to get scolded by any of the moms, not just your own. We all knew how to behave because someone was always watching.

I loved playing outside, especially since my best friend, Leola, lived right next door. We were always together, playing our favorite games: jacks, hopscotch, or jump rope. In the evenings, all the moms would hang out in lawn chairs, burning rags to keep the mosquitoes away, while us children took over the street playing dodgeball. I was always the one in charge when we played, no question about it. That leadership side of mine came out early. I was the boss, and funny enough, everyone went along with it! We had such a great time together, even though the world around us was full of prejudice and challenges.

We had to walk more than a mile to get to the nearest Black school, even though there was a White school a few blocks from our house. When a Black elementary school was finally built in our neighborhood, it felt like a small victory. But deep down, we knew the truth: We still were not welcome in the spaces that were considered "better." Sometimes, Daddy would drive us to school in the mornings, especially if it was raining or really cold. There were no sidewalks along the street on our walk to school, just a busy main road with lots of cars passing by. These days, most parents could not imagine letting their five- and seven-year-old children do that: out there all alone so early in the morning. But back then, that was normal for the Black children in the neighborhood.

I felt the sting of prejudice in White communities and within my own. As a darker-skinned, skinny Black girl, I was judged unfairly, even by other Black folks. My light-skinned siblings, with their features that society seemed to prefer, were treated differently than I was. They got more attention and praise, while I often felt invisible. Growing up as the darkest-skinned kid in my family wasn't easy. I heard all the cruel nicknames. Children would tease me, calling me "Black Olive Oyl," comparing me to Olive Oyl from the Popeye cartoons. It was rough, but my parents were my biggest supporters. They always showered me with compliments and reminded me how beautiful I was. Their opinion mattered much more to me than anyone else's, so I held onto that. But still, those early experiences were hurtful.

Any time family members visited us, they would gush over my sister's beauty and her long, black hair. She really was beautiful, but sometimes their comments would sting. I even had an aunt who nicknamed me "Betsy" after a black cow. She would tease that I was cuter than Betsy because I was smaller and had dimples, and everyone around would laugh. I would even laugh, because I knew my auntie loved me. She had lighter-skin, with hazel eyes and naturally blonde hair. Back then, it was normal to make jokes about dark skin. That kind of talk had been passed down through generations, rooted in the prejudices of slavery. Knowing that White people held some of these same beliefs made me wonder why Black people would tease me and others who had darker skin. Their actions taught me that discrimination is how others treat you, as well as how you see yourself.

Back then, being called "Black" felt like an insult, something nobody wanted to hear. Children sometimes called each other names like "Black Sambo," which was a serious insult back then. Up until about 1968, being called "Black" was anything but a compliment. You did not refer to yourself as Black. But by 1968, everything started to change. That was the year James Brown released his song, "Say It Loud, I am Black, and I am Proud," and it hit like a wake-up call. Around the same time, Tommie Smith and John Carlos, two Olympic athletes, raised their fists in protest against racial injustice and discrimination after winning medals in the 200-meter sprint. They wore black gloves and socks as a symbol of defiance. Suddenly, saying you were Black was not an insult anymore, it was a statement of pride.

The Civil Rights Movement was driving change everywhere, and being proud to call yourself Black was the new message. I was never ashamed of being Black, though. My self-esteem was rock solid because my parents always made me feel special. But it felt great to see the shift of people embracing their Blackness with pride instead of shame. It was a powerful time to be part of something bigger.

School became both my safe space and my challenge. Somehow, I found strength there. Academics and extracurriculars were my armor. I threw myself into music, sports, and cheerleading, proving to myself (and maybe to others) that no bias could define me or my worth.

The biggest test came when it was time to choose a high school to attend. Mama had her heart set on Hamilton High School. In 1966, Hamilton was the most prestigious Black school in Memphis. It was where all the affluent Black families sent their children, and let's be real, being lighter skinned didn't hurt. My sister went there and barely graduated, but her light skin made it a little easier for her socially. For Mama, Hamilton was the obvious choice. For me? Absolutely not.

I already knew I wanted to go to Booker T. Washington (BTW) High School because my best friends LuVelma Robinson and Ruby Jackson were going there. It felt more welcoming, more real. Plus, they had an awesome football team, and that sealed the deal for me! My mind was made up. BTW was where I belonged.

This wasn't about rebelling or trying to be difficult, even if it might have seemed that way. It came down to this: Hamilton did not feel like a place for me. It felt exclusive, like it wasn't built for someone who looked like me: darker skin and from a working-class family. I couldn't picture myself fitting into a world that seemed made for the children of teachers, doctors, or people who had the "right" look. That wasn't my world, and I didn't want to spend four years pretending it could be. My parents were not teachers or doctors; they were laborers — mama a maid and daddy a factory worker. Their jobs were not the kind Hamilton seemed to celebrate. I didn't want to spend my high school years feeling like an outsider. So, I stood my ground. BTW was where I belonged, and no one was going to convince me otherwise.

I knew my parents wouldn't support my choice, especially Mama. Asking her for permission was pointless. Her "No" was basically law when she didn't like something. But I wasn't about to give up. If I wanted this to happen, I had to handle it myself. That summer, I marched into the Board of Education offices, confidently filled out the transfer form, and signed Mama's name. Bold move? Sure. But that wasn't anything new for me. I had been writing checks for her and signing her name for years. This was just one more signature. Obviously, I didn't tell Mama or Daddy what I had done.

The bus system worked in my favor. Since we only used public transportation to get to school, my parents wouldn't know where I was headed each day. My plan was simple: By the time they would find out, it would be too late for them to stop me. Of course, there were risks. BTW wasn't exactly the safest school. It had a reputation for violence, and the stadium had even been shut down because of fights and a shooting. And there were trade-offs—I couldn't do after-school activities because the bus ride home was more than forty-five minutes. But it was totally worth it.

Reality hit me fast. Not long after school started, I ran into my first problem. A girl in gym class decided to test me, calling me names, trying to get under my skin, and eventually shoving me into a fight. I wasn't about to back down. That fight earned me a trip straight to the principal's office. I figured I could handle it. What I did not see coming was the principal calling Mama at work. As I sat in Mr. Springer's office, I watched him pick up the phone and start dialing. My heart was pounding before he even spoke. I heard him ask, "Can I speak to Mrs. Nervie Scales?" *Oh no!* I knew I was in for it. Then he said, "I am the principal at Booker T. Washington High School, and I need to talk to her briefly about her daughter." Talk about a sinking feeling. I wished the floor would swallow me up right then and there.

He waited silently for a moment, and then I heard him continue, "Mrs. Scales, your daughter has gotten into trouble at school today. If possible, could you come to the school to pick her up and speak with me?" My stomach was making flips as he listened to her response. Then he said, "Yes, Martha Scales. That's your daughter's name, is it not? No, ma'am, this is not Hamilton High. She's here in my office now. Would you like to speak with her?"

He motioned for me to come over, handing me the phone. "Mama," I started, "I can explain . . ."

Before I could get another word out, she cut me off, yelling, "Give the phone back to him!" I quickly handed it over to Mr. Springer and shuffled back to the chair, sinking into it with a heavy sigh. I already knew I was in deep trouble, not so much for the fight, but for lying about the school I was going to. As I sat there waiting for Mama to show up, my mind raced, trying to figure out how I would talk my way out of this. I knew Mama would be furious, and without Daddy around, I had no clue what kind of punishment was headed my way.

It felt like an hour before she arrived, though it was probably more like thirty minutes. When Mama walked in, my stomach fell. I glanced at her but couldn't bring myself to make full eye contact. I could feel her fury radiating off of her. She sat down across from Mr. Springer, while I was in another corner of the office, trying to disappear into the chair. Mr. Springer motioned for me to sit next to Mama at his desk, and I knew I was done for. Her face was exactly what I expected: pure rage. Mama's eyes burned holes right through me as she demanded to know how I had even managed to enroll at BTW.

Then, Mr. Springer pulled out the transfer form with her "signature." Yeah, I was toast. The look she gave me sent instant chills through my entire body. I was caught, with no way out, and I knew there was no smoothing this over.

Despite everything, Mr. Springer actually saw something in me that day. He looked over my transcripts and, even after the fight, decided not to suspend me. But he didn't let me off easily. He told me straight up, "Starting trouble like this could cause more trouble with other girls once they think you're a fighter." His expression was a mix of seriousness and concern for my safety. "You could really get hurt and struggle at this school." I didn't say it at the time, but I appreciated how he handled it.

Mama was not having any of it. Right there in his office, she cut him off and said, "She's not coming back." Then, she turned to me, gave me a sharp look, and said, "You are going to Hamilton, whether you like it or not." No discussion, no options.

The car ride home was brutal. I slumped so far into the back seat I might as well have vanished, silently praying Mama would hold it together until we got home. She did not put up with disrespect, and I knew I had crossed a major line. As soon as we walked through the door, Daddy got straight to it: "Why did you do it?" That was my moment. I let it all out: the judgment I would have felt at Hamilton, the cliques, the lighter-skinned girls, and how I would never feel like I belonged. But Daddy was not buying my excuses. He hit me with a steady, firm, "How do you know that?"

I didn't have a good answer, but I begged him to hear me out. I told him Booker T. Washington was where I needed to be. Mama was not having it either. She was convinced BTW was not safe.

"Sam, they are gonna kill her over there," she said. "She's got too big of a mouth, and those girls don't play."

Despite her pleas, Daddy must have seen something in what I was saying because he cut a deal. He looked at me and said, "I'll let you go back, but only if you keep your grades up and stay out of trouble. One mess-up, and you are going to Hamilton." Then he added, "Your mother is right. You need to keep your mouth shut and no more fights. You could get hurt, so you had better make some friends and stay out of trouble. Do you hear me?"

I felt so relieved. "Yes, Daddy, I promise," I said.

Mama was still mad though. I could hear her arguing with Daddy in the back room that evening. But I knew Daddy's decision was final. I didn't take that win lightly. I might not have handled it perfectly, but I kept my promise. No fights, no drama, just focus. When I walked across the stage at Booker T. Washington High School in 1969, I was a proud graduate. That time in my life was about figuring out where I fit in while navigating racism, colorism, class, and identity. Choosing BTW was a lesson in taking risks, even when people doubted me. It showed me that hearing "No" does not always mean the door is closed; it's the beginning of a negotiation.

The late '60s were a wild mix of big changes and deep frustrations in America. The Civil Rights Movement was in full swing, but in Memphis, progress felt slow. The "Whites Only" signs might have come down, but the fight was far from over. I was determined to make a difference. I was so angry at the pervasive White supremacist mentality. I started thinking more radically, drawn to the ideas of Stokely Carmichael and the Black Panthers including co-founders Huey Newton and Bobby Seale, and moving further away from Martin Luther King Jr's peaceful approach. Afros were in style, and of course, I had to have one. Mama was not a fan of that hairstyle, but for me, the afro was more than a hairstyle, it was my way of protesting, of standing in the middle of all the chaos as the Civil Rights Movement exploded around me.

Then, there was my eleventh-grade World History teacher, Nat D. Williams. He completely changed how I saw the world. On the first day of class, he walked in and said, "We are not bothering with the usual history textbooks. Leave them at home. We are going to learn our history—Black history—woven into American history."

Mr. Williams did not brush off my fiery opinions or frustration. Instead, he pushed me to think deeper. One day, he gave me an assignment to write about ending segregation and discrimination. I had some pretty strong opinions, shaped by things like having to walk a mile to elementary school even though there was a school just two blocks away. Or being sent to the back of the doctor's office. These experiences left a brutal mark on my psyche.

My essay started off pretty radical. It was not about bowing down, praying, or waiting for change, it was about standing up for our rights and fighting for them if we had to. I wrote about how this new generation of young Black Americans was not going to accept the same treatment our parents endured. I believed education was our key to power. I said we needed to run for elective office so we could make real change. I didn't think we should go to jail without a fight. I wrote that we should walk into White neighborhoods, eat at their restaurants, and show them we are not second-class citizens; we are first class. My essay was a mix of anger and strategy. I wanted us to push back against injustice with radical protests, but with a plan to achieve equality.

Honestly, I wanted to strip the power from White people who thought they were superior and make them feel the injustice and prejudice we'd faced for so long. My essay was emotional, raw, and personal. A lot of it came from the anger I felt watching how my parents were treated. I hated seeing my mother, who was much older than some of the White people she worked with, being called by her first name while she had to address them as "Mrs. Smith" or "Mr. Jones" and say, "Yes ma'am" or "No sir." They should have been addressing her as their senior—with "Yes ma'am" or "Mrs. Scales."

I wrote more than fifteen pages. After class, Mr. Williams pulled me aside for a chat. To my surprise, he told me he'd read the whole thing and wanted to dive deeper into it with me.

"Martha," he said, "You'll never defeat discrimination or segregation from the outside. Radicalism will only lead to more radicalism. If you want real change, you have got to get inside the system and change it from within."

Those words reframed how I saw justice, activism, and my own power to make a difference. His words stuck with me and fueled me to keep fighting for justice, equality, and respect, but in a smarter, more strategic way. Mr. Williams warned me not to let anger derail my success. He shared stories about how discrimination had held back his own career, but how he also believed my generation had a brighter future.

He helped me understand that being too radical could keep me on the outside of the spaces where real change happens. He reminded me that hatred only creates barriers and limits access to people who need to change their perspectives.

"Keep educating yourself, Martha, so you'll be ready to enter environments at a much higher professional level where decisions will be made by people who might hold prejudice views—management positions, industry organizations, social environments, and community engagements," he explained.

"Once you are inside of these environments, that's when you can become influential and start breaking barriers and changing minds," Mr. Williams said. "Never forget that you are Black and where you came from, and as you open doors, always reach back and bring others with you.

"Never feel inferior, because you deserve to be in those rooms as much as anyone else, no matter who they are," he said.

He wanted me to understand that belonging is about me knowing my worth and never feeling intimidated. That's how to bring about real change: from within the system. If you are too radical, you'll never get in the door, and then you cannot be effective. But once you are inside, you can use your personality and intelligence to confront injustice and create meaningful change, not with anger or hatred, but with purpose.

That conversation completely shifted how I thought about moving forward. I didn't have to give up my beliefs to tackle discrimination. Mr. Williams taught me history and how to make history. Then, he did something amazing: He gave me a few minutes on his WDIA radio show to share my thoughts on the racial tensions in Memphis. It was such a bold move back then, and for the first time, I felt like my voice carried beyond my friends and family. That opportunity lit a fire in me.

When Dr. King came to Memphis to lead the sanitation workers' protest, I knew I had to be there. Mr. Williams had already prepared me to believe I could make a difference. Our generation was ready for change, and it was time to make sure our voices were heard. My mom—always supportive but always worried—gave me her usual warning: "Be careful, and don't let that mouth of yours get you into trouble." She said it with a smile, knowing there was no stopping me once I made up my mind.

On March 28, 1968, I walked out of Booker T. Washington High School with dozens of other students and joined the march on Beale Street. The energy was incredible. There was so much hope for change in the air. We sang protest songs, including "Henry Loeb Gotta Go," aimed at the mayor who refused to recognize basic rights for sanitation workers. But as we got closer to Main Street, everything changed. Suddenly, there was chaos. Tear gas filled the air, and people started running in every direction. It was terrifying. By the time we made it to Clayborn Temple AME Church, I was scared and confused about how a peaceful march had gone so wrong.

Later, we learned that a few agitators had broken windows and the police responded with violence, completely overshadowing the purpose of the march. When I finally got back to school, I wasn't able to take the bus back home because the mayor had shut down the bus system out of concern that riots might erupt. Our principal told us to go straight home. Luckily, Mr. Robinson, LuVelma's dad, picked us up. When I got home, Mama hugged me tight.

"I didn't want you to go, but thank God you are okay," she said.

"Somebody has to help Dr. King make these changes," I told her. Even then, I knew this was not his fight alone, it was ours, all of the young people who believed a change was necessary, all of the Black people who had been ignored and pushed to the margins of society.

Dr. King came back to Memphis in April, but he never got to finish what he started. His assassination on April 4th shattered the country. It felt personal to me. I couldn't stop crying, thinking about how Mama and I had talked about him fixing the injustices we lived with. And now, he was gone. I couldn't help but wonder, *Will we ever see justice? Will discrimination in America ever really end?* A few days later, on April 8th, we marched again, this time to honor Dr. King. It was heartbreaking, but at the same time, there was a feeling of determination in the air. As we marched through downtown Memphis, the Freedom Singers' song, "Ain't Gonna Let Nobody Turn Me Around" echoed everywhere. Those words hit me hard. Even now, they are with me, reminding me to keep pushing forward no matter what life throws at me.

Mr. Williams taught me that fighting injustice is about having a plan. My mom showed me how to hold onto love, even when the world tries to replace it with hate. Dr. King's legacy gave me hope, reminding me that even slow progress is still progress if we stay committed. Several of these lessons became the foundation for G.U.T.S.: the grit to face obstacles, the understanding to look beyond anger, the tenacity to create change, and the strength to keep going, even when it feels impossible. Those moments of protest, reflection, and growth in Memphis planted the seeds for everything I have done since. The fight for justice and equality is not over, not even close. But I carry with me this unshakable belief: No matter how deep discrimination runs, it cannot dim the light of someone determined to make a difference.

Facing Discrimination at Work

Years later, when I started working, I often found myself as the only Black person in mostly White spaces. Mr. Williams's advice stayed with me during those times. Instead of meeting discrimination with anger or confrontation, I chose to educate and engage. It was not easy, but it was worth it. When a colleague said something inappropriate or ignorant, I would stay calm and ask, "Why do you feel that way?" or "What do you mean by that?" Those became my go-to questions. If things started to get tense, I would lighten the mood with humor or respond firmly but kindly. I would say something like, "I know you didn't mean to be insulting, because you are better than that," with a smile.

Most of the time, it worked. A lot of people didn't realize their words or actions were biased, they were merely repeating things they'd heard or believed. Those private conversations often led to real "aha" moments, and I got to see coworkers start to question and break down their own prejudices. That's how I learned to create change from the inside. By collaborating, volunteering, and having honest conversations, I was able to shift opinions and help build a more inclusive environment. Every person I reached added to the ripple effect, spreading understanding far beyond our workplace.

My childhood lessons, my high school protests, and the guidance of incredible mentors showed me that real change starts with positioning yourself within the environment that you are trying to change. To fight injustice, you have to choose courage, purpose, and empathy. I am proud of the work I have done in this area. Whether in offices, communities, or my personal relationships, my work has helped shift perspectives and brought Dr. King's dream a little closer to reality.

If you are facing injustice, here's my advice:

- **Be courageous:** Confront prejudice with confidence while responding thoughtfully and respectfully.
- **Lead through actions:** Demonstrate a better way by embodying kindness and authenticity. These approaches achieve far more than direct confrontation.
- **Stay authentic:** Engage in spaces where you can create meaningful change but never compromise your true self.
- **Change begins with conversation:** Meaningful conversations are the foundation of progress.

Resilience is about surviving injustice and turning challenges into opportunities to grow, learn, and push progress forward, for everyone. Dr. King could not fix every problem we face, but his legacy lives on in every ripple of change we create today. My ability to create change is rooted in the foundation laid by Mama, Daddy, Mr. Williams, and so many others who shaped me.

Over time, the way I fought against injustice and discrimination shifted to something more sustainable and impactful. I learned to let go of anger and lean into action. I stopped pushing back and started persuading. I moved away from conflict and toward connection. I didn't lose the fire in me; I learned to use that fire in a smarter way to educate and influence. Turning hate into humanity opened doors for the change I wanted to see, for myself and for others who might never have thought differently without a real person challenging their biases.

One of the biggest lessons I have learned is that fighting for justice does not always mean being the loudest voice in the room or on the streets. Sometimes, the most radical move is pulling up a chair at the table and forcing them to see you, hear you, and learn from you. That's where real change happens.

Lessons in G.U.T.S.

Mama taught me that if you are going to fight injustice, you have got to have G.U.T.S. It took me years to understand, but now it's become my guide for facing discrimination head-on. Let me break it down for you:

G — Gratitude: I am deeply thankful to Nat D. Williams for reshaping my mindset and equipping me with the wisdom to address injustices and discrimination more strategically. His guidance taught me the power of working within the system, where these issues often take root, and showed me that hatred only builds walls and hinders meaningful dialogue with those who need to shift their perspectives. This early lesson gave me the tools to drive impactful changes within my sphere of influence and to help pave the way for future generations of Black professionals. Mr. Williams's mentorship and teachings were instrumental in laying the foundation for G.U.T.S.

U — Unity: Change is never a solo act. It thrives on connection, whether that's within a group, a movement, or even with the unwavering support of one trusted friend. Unity is the foundation of strength. A united front commands attention, compelling others to stop, reflect, and take notice. Unity wields a power that cannot be overlooked. The protests and marches in Memphis stand as a testament to this truth, where the collective voice of many shone a light on injustices and ultimately led to meaningful, successful change.

T — Trustworthiness: Fighting injustice is a draining journey; I know that firsthand. There were countless moments when I felt like giving up, ready to walk away from it all. But through those struggles, I have come to understand the power of staying honest and self-reflective, even when it's uncomfortable. We all carry biases, and acknowledging them is a crucial step forward. Nat D. Williams once saw in me what I struggled to see in myself: a loving heart and a genuine commitment to confronting injustice. That recognition taught me that being truthful about your thoughts and intentions can be deeply healing. Honesty begins within. To create meaningful change, you must first know yourself. Search your character, align it with truth, and let purpose guide your actions.

S — Spirituality: Mama always said, "Baby, you cannot fight hate with hate." And she was right. Like Dr. King taught us, only love can drive out hate. But love does not mean giving up the fight, it means fighting smarter. Make them *see* you. Make them *feel* you. My spirituality has always kept me grounded, reminding me that love is action, even when it feels like the world does not deserve it.

If you are in this fight, remember to lead with G.U.T.S. It'll take you further than you think. This fight is not about today; it's about tomorrow. It is for the next generation of dreamers, doers, and innovators who try to make their way in a tough world. Change does not wait; it's happening now, through us, because of us. What part will you play in shaping what's next? I hear Mama's words every time I step up to the challenge. Dr. King's dream *can* be real, but it's going to take all of us standing in empathy, bravery, and a whole lot of G.U.T.S.

CHAPTER 4

No Does Not Mean No

*No does not mean "No," it means you have to find another
way to make it happen.*

When someone tells you "No," how do you respond? Is it a conclusion, or is it a challenge? For me, "No" has never been a stopping point; it's always been an invitation to find another way to achieve my goals. Every "No" can be an opportunity to build determination and resilience and turn a perceived roadblock into a launching pad for success.

Early in my life, I encountered countless noes that could have easily discouraged me. Instead, I made each one a learning experience. Each rejection, misstep, or closed door became an opportunity to refine my approach, gain insights, and build a stronger foundation for future attempts. "No" never closed the door for me, it merely pointed me to a different one and taught me to think bigger, work harder, and most importantly, never put limits on what I could achieve. Seeing setbacks as opportunities for growth can completely transform the path to your goals.

The Shorthand Classroom Battle

Attending Booker T. Washington High School proved to me that I belonged in a world that often doubted me. Back then, technical skills like shorthand were essential for careers in administration. So, I signed up for a shorthand class, only to face a no the moment I did.

Ms. Wilson, my teacher, looked at me, realized that I was left-handed, and told me bluntly, "You cannot take this class." Her reasoning was simple but deeply flawed: The stenographer's pad was designed for right-handed individuals, and she believed I would never be able to keep up. She didn't give me a chance to prove otherwise. Instead, she handed me a note instructing me to go to the office and sign up for another class.

I took the note to the office, but not to drop the class. Instead, I went to the principal, Mr. Springer, and explained the discriminatory nature of Ms. Wilson's decision. I told him I deserved to try, regardless of what she assumed about my abilities. Mr. Springer agreed and let Ms. Wilson know I could stay in the class. Shortly after, I returned to the shorthand class and faced Ms. Wilson's icy demeanor head-on. I saw in her expression that she wanted me to fail, but I was not going to give her the satisfaction.

The initial challenges were real. Shorthand was not easy with the stenographer's pad. I was slower than my peers, and Ms. Wilson made no effort to hide her delight in pointing it out. But instead of giving up, I found another way. During one class, I noticed that the albums she used to dictate our practice exercises had a public library stamp on the label. That evening, I visited the downtown public library and checked out several albums. I began practicing every night, starting with slower speeds and working my way up. Within weeks, my speed and accuracy improved dramatically.

During the first semester's final exam, Ms. Wilson dictated at progressively faster speeds. I was the only student still transcribing at one hundred and twenty words per minute, shockingly surpassing the expectations she had set for me. After that day, even Ms. Wilson had to acknowledge her mistake, and she began encouraging me to perfect my skills. Her shift in attitude was proof of my ability and the power of perseverance.

That experience taught me a crucial lesson about the importance of self-advocacy and resourcefulness. When someone underestimates you or tells you no, it's not necessarily about your actual abilities, it's often about their limited perception of what is possible. But here is the thing: Nobody is entitled to define your limits except you. My willingness to problem-solve, be persistent, and think creatively transformed my shorthand experience. Mr. Williams had taught me that I could always deal with prejudices with intellect rather than anger. Although Ms. Wilson didn't provide me with resources or mentorship, I looked at the situation analytically and asked myself, "What tools are available to help me succeed?" That mindset shaped the way I approached challenges for the rest of my life.

From that one lesson in the shorthand classroom, I learned to approach difficulties in my career and personal life with calm, composed strategy. Instead of being overwhelmed by obstacles, I learned to dissect them, understand their components, and create a plan to overcome them. When you see a setback as a puzzle to solve rather than an insurmountable barrier, you empower yourself to move forward no matter what the odds.

No is a powerful word, but it doesn't have to be a dead end. Instead, it can be an opportunity to discover the breadth of your potential and to grow beyond what you might imagine. Each no is an opportunity to sharpen your determination, refine your strategies, and shape a path that is uniquely yours. Resilience endures a setback, and it also uses the setback as a steppingstone to greater achievements.

From that point forward, I started to see every no as an opportunity to fuel my determination, pushing me to find creative solutions when traditional pathways were blocked. I developed the confidence to stand up for myself, even in the face of authority. By recognizing that I had the power to change the narrative and take control of my destiny, I discovered how resilient I truly was.

More importantly, my success in shorthand became a metaphor for larger life challenges. It reminded me that the tools for success often exist right in front of you, even if others cannot—or will not—point them out. Sometimes, it takes a willingness to dig deeper, work harder, and believe in yourself when the odds are stacked against you. That mindset took G.U.T.S. and became the foundation for every future no I would face; and trust me, there were many more to come.

My refusal to take no for an answer didn't stop after high school. Later, when I enrolled at Tennessee State University, I chose business as my major, still uncertain of where my path would lead. But because I lacked focus during my freshman year—both academically and with following dorm rules—I was sent home, having lost sight of my goals.

It was a tough setback, but I was determined to continue my education. So, I enrolled at the newly integrated two-year college, State Technical Institute. There, I initially studied accounting but quickly realized it was not for me. Computer science, a field recommended by a friend, piqued my interest. I saw this major as exciting and innovative, offering opportunities that could overcome racial bias by emphasizing new abilities and specialized expertise, which were in short supply in the workforce.

Once again, I heard the dreaded no. The academic advisors told me my ACT math scores were not high enough to succeed in computer science. It felt like another roadblock shaped by systemic inequities. I mean, think about it, Black students like me were stuck with outdated textbooks all through school. From elementary to high school, we got the hand-me-down books from White schools, and they were years behind. How could academic testing ever be fair in a setup like that?

But I was not about to let that no define me. I thought back to everything Mr. Williams taught me about advocacy and standing up for what is right. So, I pushed back. I told them that if I failed, it would not be because I was not capable, it would be because the system had failed me. I demanded a chance. And guess what? Before long, I was sitting in my first computer science class.

With intense focus and effort, I worked tirelessly toward success. It was not easy. I had to study harder than other students who'd arrived with a foundation of study in this area. I also made the tough decision to skip social events, and I wrestled with self-doubt. However, something about programming and problem-solving ignited a passion within me that I had not felt before. It was as though I had finally found a path that aligned with both my curiosity and my determination. I threw myself fully into my studies, immersing myself in coding languages, logic design, and systems analysis.

Soon, my hard work began to pay off. I excelled in my classes, often finding myself ahead of my classmates in understanding complex concepts. My persistence began to shift opinions, and I gained the respect and trust of my peers and instructors. By the end of the first semester, I completed the courses with an A average, proving to myself and to those who doubted me that their "no" held no weight against my determination.

Success in the classroom didn't always translate to acceptance in the professional world, particularly in Memphis. At the time, the industry was still in its infancy. Internship and employment opportunities were limited, especially for Black professionals, and even more so for Black women. Every interview felt like a trial, made worse by the burden I felt to prove myself twice over: once as a woman and again as a Black professional. Doubts about my abilities, rooted in both my race and gender, lingered like a fragile yet persistent shadow. Despite going on numerous interviews, I could not secure a job in Memphis that allowed me to utilize my newly developed skills. It was in this moment of frustration and reflection that I realized my dreams could not be fulfilled in Memphis.

I felt trapped, unsure how to escape the harsh reality that my aspirations had come to a standstill. It seemed another setback had emerged, threatening to derail my progress. Still, I held on to hope.

I asked God why this was happening. In my search for answers, I would sit and cry while talking to Mama about my disappointments. She'd encourage me to trust in God. "Baby, God knows what's going on," she'd say. "He'll open some doors. Don't give up. God is always in charge."

"But when, Mama? When?" I'd asked her.

Despite my disappointment in the face of adversity, the power of G.U.T.S. continued to shape my principles and guide my decisions.

Lessons in G.U.T.S.

People may try to define your limits, but that doesn't mean you have to accept them. Whether it's a teacher telling you your left-handedness is a barrier, or an advisor saying your math scores preclude success, those noes are only opinions, not facts. The next time you are told "No," pause and ask yourself if it's truly the end of the road or if it's a chance to find another way.

With G.U.T.S., all things are possible. Refuse to settle for what others believe you cannot achieve. You define your destiny. Turn their no into your undeniable yes. The triumphs I have shared in this chapter are rooted in the principles of the G.U.T.S. framework, which has guided me through every obstacle:

G — Gratitude: Gratitude reminds us to cherish the opportunities we are given, even when wrapped in challenges. I was grateful for the chance to prove myself, even though it came through adversity.

U — Unity: No one achieves success alone. From Mr. Springer's advocacy to my friend's advice about computer science, unity played a key role in my journey. Building collaborative relationships strengthens your foundation for success.

T — Trustworthiness: Staying true to my values and proving my reliability reinforced others' trust in me while strengthening my trust in myself.

S — Spirituality: Spirituality helped me find a purpose beyond myself. My mom always reminded me not to give up on God because He's the one in control. Every setback I faced was actually building the foundation of my faith. That faith gave me the strength to bounce back and stay focused on my bigger goals.

CHAPTER 5

Overcoming Setbacks and Disappointments

Patience, persistence, patience, persistence. Never give up on the dream. Revise it, change the measurements, revamp the plan, but don't give up on the dream.

In addition to facing the challenges of changing my major from accounting to computer science at State Technical Institute, life presented an unexpected reality for me. During my second year, I found out that I was pregnant.

At first, the news of my unexpected pregnancy left me completely overwhelmed with the thought of being a single parent at age eighteen. I was filled with a mix of emotions—fear, sadness, and frustration—but also joy and gratitude for the new life that would soon make its way into the world. Having a baby at this stage of my life was not part of the plan I had carefully envisioned for myself. All I could think about was how it would affect my education, my career, and my ability to provide for myself, and now, for my child.

One afternoon, I sat alone in my car outside of the OB/GYN doctor's office with tears streaming down my face. The weight of the responsibility ahead felt crushing, and I couldn't help but feel as though I had failed before I had even begun. It was a moment of profound despair, as all the dreams and goals I had worked so hard to pursue seemed to slip further out of reach.

When I told Ricky, my child's father, about the pregnancy, his reaction crushed me. I had met Ricky in the spring before I left for Tennessee State. He lived in my neighborhood and was friends with Charles, a friend of mine who lived up the street and also liked me. Ricky had an incredible smile that totally won me over. At the time, he was starting his senior year in high school. His mom was a homemaker, and his dad was a minister who also ran an upholstery shop where Ricky worked. Sometimes, I would go over to help him out with a few jobs. We had so much fun together during those times.

What I didn't know—at least not at first—was that Ricky was also dating a girl from Southside High School. He managed to juggle the two relationships pretty easily since she didn't live near us. When I found out later, it hit me hard. Charles had tried to warn me about it, but I didn't believe him; I thought he was just trying to get me to break up with Ricky.

When I dropped out of Tennessee State University and came home from college, Ricky and I started dating again. That's when he told me about the other girlfriend. But even after that, he kept coming over, and we kept going out. I would go to his house, he would come to mine; it all felt normal, even though deep down, I knew something wasn't right. I was busy with school and working nights, so I didn't have much time to think deeply about the situation. But I knew he was seeing both of us. Still, I convinced myself he loved me more and that it would eventually end with her. What I didn't know was that they had been dating for more than two years.

Then came the night everything changed. Ricky and I were sitting in his car in my parents' driveway when I told him I was pregnant. He pulled out his pack of Kool cigarettes, lit one, shook his head, and said, "Wow."

That's it. Then he asked, "How far along are you?"

I told him, "About two months."

He flicked the cigarette out the window, looked at me, and said the words that crushed me: "Martha, my other girlfriend is pregnant too. She's having my child, and I'm going to marry her."

I was stunned, heartbroken. I managed to choke out, "What am I supposed to do?" I didn't expect an answer, but I needed something, anything, to make sense of this.

"You're really going to do this to me? I didn't make this baby alone, Ricky. You were as involved in this as I was!" Tears were streaming down my face as I looked at him. "She's having your baby, Ricky. So am I. So am I."

But he didn't care. He didn't even flinch. He just looked at me, completely cold, and said, "I'm committed to Shirley, and marrying her is the right thing to do."

He stared out the window, emotionless, like none of this mattered to him: not me, not our baby, nothing. I couldn't believe it. My chest felt tight, like my heart was being ripped apart. His betrayal hurt, and so did the realization that I was on my own. My future, my baby's future, was now uncertain. I felt scared, overwhelmed, and completely lost. All I could do at that moment was cry.

But Ricky was not done. He had to add one more punch to the gut: "How do I even know the baby is mine?"

I just stared at him, completely floored. "How could you say that, Ricky? You *know* better," I said, my voice shaking. I had been faithful to him, even when he had not been to me.

His denial was not about me, it was about him trying to escape the reality of having two women pregnant at the same time. It was clear he was not ready to face the mess he'd created, and I immediately understood where he was headed with this. He didn't have the courage to admit to his other girlfriend that he had been cheating on her all along, so denial became his easy escape from disappointing her.

As he denied that my child was his, my mind raced: *What will Mama think? How will I manage this alone? What am I going to do?* These questions consumed me as I screamed and cried, our argument escalating with each of his denials. The argument hit its peak when his voice got louder, completely drowning me out. Instead of listening to me, he continued to deny that the baby was his. After nearly an hour of arguing, I couldn't take it anymore. My chest felt heavy as each of his words crushed me. I knew I couldn't win this fight. Shaking, my face covered in tears, I grabbed my purse and stormed out. The cool night air hit me as I walked toward the door to enter the house, feeling totally numb.

The moment I walked inside, Mama knew something was up. She was in the kitchen, prepping some stewed apples for her apple jam, and the second she saw me, she stopped what she was doing. Mama was not the overly emotional type, but her face told me she could tell that something was seriously wrong. She never liked Ricky. She had her reasons, like how he would show up at the house and just sit in the driveway instead of coming inside. She always said, "A decent man would at least come in and say hello to your parents, not just honk for you to run out." So yeah, she didn't think much of him from the start.

It was late, around 9:30 p.m., and I knew I had to tell her that night. After splashing some water on my face in the bathroom, I went back into the kitchen, staring at the floor, barely able to lift my head. I sat down, trying to catch my breath, but the words spilled out between sobs. Finally, I blurted out, "Mama, I'm pregnant … and Ricky's denying the baby is his."

Her face showed a whole range of emotions, from shock to worry, and then that determined, no-nonsense look she always had when she meant business. She pulled me into a hug, whispering that it was going to be okay, but I could feel how tense she was. I needed her support so badly, but all I could think about was how much my life was about to change.

Daddy wasn't home because he worked a second job and always came home very late. I knew I had to tell him myself first thing in the morning, before Mama did, so I woke up early to make sure I could sit with him at breakfast. I was beyond nervous. Daddy had always had such high hopes for me, and this was going to be a huge disappointment. I also knew how proud he was of our family. He believed in doing the right thing, always. I had no idea how he'd react when I told him Ricky was denying the baby was his. Would he grab his shotgun and pay Ricky a visit? Probably not, but I wouldn't have been surprised. Still, I knew one thing for sure: my daddy loved me. No matter what, he'd find a way to dry my tears and pick me back up, even if this broke his heart a little.

When I finally told him, his face stayed calm, and his voice was steady. "We cannot make a man be a man," he said firmly. "A decent man will take responsibility, no matter what. He can't marry two women, but he sure as hell knows that this is his child. The least he can do is own up to it."

Then, Daddy went to his room, and I followed him, still crying. He hugged me tight and told me, "Don't worry, you'll be fine. It's okay." Those words hit me hard. They were simple and exactly what I needed. In that moment, I felt like I could face whatever was coming. Mama and Daddy still loved me, and somehow, that gave me enough strength to believe I would get through this.

Going to school while pregnant was one of the hardest things I have ever done. The emotional weight of Ricky's rejection constantly hung over me. Most days, I felt utterly defeated, wondering how I could possibly keep going. My heart was shattered. Juggling the physical demands of pregnancy with the rigorous expectations of my studies stretched me to my limits. Each classroom lecture, each late-night study session, was accompanied by an undercurrent of sadness and doubt. Despite the heartbreaking and overwhelming pressure, I found a strength within me that I had not known existed. I pressed on, one step at a time, determined to create a better future for myself and my baby. Even with a broken heart, I refused to give up.

While at State Technical Institute, I had a hard time landing an internship. I am sure it was because I was Black. All the White students were given preference over any of the Black students. It was the second year the school had been integrated. Rather than fighting the systems by pushing to get an internship, I accepted that this was just how it was going to be in Memphis. I had become immune to rejection and prejudices, and my hope was quickly fading. All I wanted to do was leave, but I saw no way out. So, I took a part-time job. Even though I was pregnant, I knew I needed to start working so I wouldn't be a financial burden on my family. My best friend LuVelma's sister worked at Collins Chapel Hospital, a Black-owned institution fighting to keep its accreditation. She shared that they were hiring for a night office clerk, so I applied for the job right away and was hired at $1.18 an hour, which was minimum wage back then.

Collins Chapel Hospital was an important part of the community, providing care to Black people who needed it, even though the hospital was struggling financially. It had a modest but welcoming vibe of determination and hope that emanated from everyone, staff and patients alike.

Working the night shift came with its challenges, especially while I was pregnant. The hospital was quieter at night, with dimmed lights and a slower pace, but there were still moments of urgency that kept me on my toes. I juggled answering calls, taking care of administrative work, and sometimes offering a kind word to people who came through the door. It wasn't easy balancing the exhaustion of pregnancy with the job while attending college full time, but I took pride in being part of the hospital's mission. The Black doctors in Memphis had come together to form the Bluff City Medical Society, and they were all registered to practice at this hospital, as well as at Methodist and Baptist hospitals.

One night, I sat in the hospital lobby, chatting with my family doctor who had known me my whole life. As we talked, he realized I was pregnant. He looked at me and, without any sugarcoating, said, "You're not going to have this baby. It doesn't make sense. You're in college, and you need to finish."

Then, his voice became firm. "This is the last thing you need. You are way too smart for this. I'll send you to someone who can take care of it." He asked how far along I was.

"A couple of months," I replied.

He nodded and said, "That's fine. I'll get you the connection tomorrow."

At the time, abortions were illegal, but plenty of people were still doing them under the radar.

Heartbroken by Ricky's rejection and his plans to marry another woman, I spiraled into a deep depression. After considering the doctor's advice, I decided to have the abortion and scheduled an appointment. Keeping the abortion plan a secret was one of the most isolating experiences of my life. I didn't share it with anyone, not even my closest friends or family. The fear of judgment and the weight of shame compelled me to carry the burden alone. Spiritually, I was deeply conflicted. My faith had always been a guiding force in my life, but at that moment, I felt lost and uncertain of how to reconcile my beliefs with the decision I had made. The truth is, I believed I was beyond redemption, yet in my lowest moment, I clung to prayer, seeking solace and guidance.

On the day of the procedure, I drove to a discreet location. Sitting in my car, I spent nearly an hour in prayer, pouring my heart out to God. As I waited, I noticed another woman leaving, flanked by two others. Suddenly, an unshakable feeling inside me refused to let me go through with it. Overcome with emotion, I started the car and drove away, tears streaming down my face, my heart weighed down with sorrow. I knew I would have to talk to my doctor and explain my decision not to go through with the abortion. Certain of his disappointment, I braced myself for criticism, but to my surprise he was kind and compassionate, even if he didn't completely understand my choice.

"You are making a big mistake," he said. "Having this baby will bring some setbacks in your life. Even still, I support your decision because I know how smart you are. You'll figure it out."

Despite his concerns, he still supported me because he understood my worth. Although he accepted my decision, he also made it clear that he thought I would eventually regret it. Even so, I appreciated his support and guidance during that time. To honor him as an advocate and aid during such a difficult time in my life, I decided that if I had a boy, I would give him my doctor's initials for his name.

When I told Mama that I had considered an abortion, she was furious with me, unable to make sense of me even considering such a thing. Daddy, on the other hand, overlooked my short-lived thoughts of giving up on the life that grew inside of me, and he reassured me that everything would be alright, that we would figure it out together. That was who he was, always ready with a comforting word whenever I faced a difficult moment.

On the night of August 26th—the same day Ricky and Shirley got married—I went into labor. That was one of the hardest days of my life. I could not stop thinking about Ricky and Shirley saying "I do" at 6:30 p.m. at her house. The man I had once loved was starting a new chapter with someone else, and it felt like too much to handle. I was overwhelmed with sadness and disappointment, and as the hours went by, the pain—both emotional and physical—grew stronger. Even with Mama and Daddy by my side, I was drowning in heartbreak. I couldn't think about anything else. The stress of it all must have triggered my labor because, before I knew it, the contractions started. It was like my body and heart were breaking all at once. Despite my heartache, my son, Adrian Fionn, was born. He arrived two months early, weighing only four and a half pounds.

Three weeks later, Adrian's weight dropped to three and a half pounds, and he developed jaundice and a kidney infection. The doctor told us his condition was critical, and he was dying. The hospital where Adrian was born lacked the necessary facilities to save him, so he had to be transferred to City Hospital for specialized care. As a new mother, I was overwhelmed with joy, fear, and an indescribable sense of helplessness. Adrian could not come home, and every passing day felt like an eternity. I was terrified for him. He looked so fragile, so tiny in the incubator, surrounded by tubes and machines. My heart ached as I sat by his side, wanting nothing more than to hold him close and protect him from everything. I prayed endlessly, asking God to spare him, to give him the strength to fight. The uncertainty was unbearable, but I clung to hope with every fiber of my being.

I could not believe he was dying. When I arrived at the hospital where they had moved him, I saw his tiny body hooked up to tubes, enclosed in an incubator. Standing outside the nursery window, I stared at him and broke down, collapsing to the floor in tears. Back then, new mothers were not allowed in the nursery, so all I could do was watch as the nurses tended to him. His face was so small, yet so painfully peaceful. It was sad see his tiny body so helpless yet comforting to know that God had spared him to live. He was framed by an array of tubes and monitors that beeped at irregular intervals. His chest rose and fell in shallow movements, as though each breath was a monumental effort.

The sight of his fragile form, swaddled in a blanket far too big for him, shattered my heart into pieces. The incubator, meant to shield him from harm, seemed instead like a cruel prison, separating him from the warmth and love I so desperately wanted to give. My mind raced with questions, each louder and more painful than the last. *Will he survive this? Have I done something wrong? Is it my fault he's here?*

I felt an overwhelming guilt, a gnawing sensation in the pit of my stomach that would not relent. Yet there were flickers of hope amid the tidal wave of fear and despair. I watched Adrian's tiny fists curl and unclench, an indication of the fight in him, a fight I believed he had inherited from me. I whispered prayers under my breath, begging for more time, for a miracle, for anything to bring him back to me healthy. Helplessness whispered words of despair to me, but I vowed not to give in. If Adrian could fight, so could I, no matter how unbearable it felt to stand by and watch, powerless to intervene.

One night after getting off of work at 11 p.m. I went to see my baby. As I gazed through the window of the nursery, praying and crying,

I suddenly crumbled to the floor. A compassionate, heavy-set Black nurse rushed over to help, gently lifting me off the floor and wrapping her thick arms around me. Through my sobs, I kept repeating, "I am so sorry. What have I done?"

She held me firmly and said, "You did not do anything. He's just a premature baby. And he's going to live."

Her compassion was exactly what I needed when I felt completely lost and broken. The way she held me—strong but gentle—reminded me that I was not alone in all the uncertainty. Her words, so calm and kind, cut through my despair and gave me hope, something I didn't think I could feel in that moment. That small act of care, her steady reassurance and warmth, became a turning point for me. It made me believe that things would be okay. It was such a powerful reminder of how much human connection and empathy can mean, especially when we are at our lowest.

I clung to her words and hugged her tightly. She looked into my eyes and said, "I work the late-night shift. Whenever I am here, come find me. I'll bring you in to feed and rock this baby back to life." Her kindness was the lifeline I desperately needed.

Although I was given six weeks for maternity leave, I needed to return to work early because I needed the money. With Adrian still in the hospital, I asked my boss if I could return to work immediately. Thankfully, she allowed it. Because the City Hospital was not far from where I worked, I could stop by before and after my shift to check on Adrian's progress. After my night shift ended at 11 p.m., I would head to the City Hospital to see my baby. On the nights my angel nurse was working, she would dress me in a patient gown, sneak me into the back of the nursery, and settle me into a rocking chair. There, I would hold my tiny son, feeding him and cradling him close. At that point, he weighed only 2.8 pounds, so fragile and small.

Those moments with Adrian in my arms were a mixture of overwhelming love, hope, and fear all intertwined. I remember the warmth of his delicate body against mine, the rhythmic rise and fall of his tiny chest as he breathed, and the way his fingers seemed impossibly small. Each heartbeat I felt through his fragile frame filled me with determination to be strong for him. Sitting in that rocking chair, time seemed to stand still and everything else disappeared. Even with all the challenges ahead, holding him gave me a sense of purpose and created a bond that grew stronger every second.

After four weeks of care, love, and determination, Adrian reached five pounds, the weight he needed to be in order to be considered out of danger and discharged from the hospital. Finally, they let me take him home, and a new chapter of my life began. As a single mother, I would have to develop a fierce resolve to balance school and work so I could create a better life for myself and my son. I promised myself I would finish my education, land a good job, and provide for Adrian on my own. He was my reason to persevere, and I was determined to give him everything he needed.

When I brought Adrian home, Mama and Daddy welcomed us with open arms. Their house was a place of warmth and stability, filled with unwavering love and support. Mama was already preparing bottles and helping me set up a space for Adrian, while Daddy could not stop smiling every time he looked at my precious baby boy. They cared for Adrian as if he were their own, making it abundantly clear that we were never alone. Ricky never showed up, not that I expected him to. And, honestly, Mama and Daddy would not have let him through the door. Their fierce protectiveness ensured Adrian would grow up in a nurturing and secure environment. Their unwavering love only deepened my determination to succeed, reminding me that family was all we truly needed. Surrounded by their care and support, I silently vowed to honor everything they had done for us.

I began searching for a new job, going through interview after interview, but I couldn't secure a position utilizing my newly acquired computer skills from my college courses. It was incredibly disheartening. As a single mother, this felt like another major life setback. After all the hard work I had put into learning computer programming, I still couldn't find a job in Memphis. These challenges started to take a toll on me mentally, leaving me uncertain about my next steps. With increased responsibilities and the need for a full-time job, I decided to apply for secretarial positions.

The newspaper was filled with job listings for law firms, banks, and other companies. Certain I was a strong candidate, I submitted countless applications. Each time, I would take their tests, excel with flying colors, and leave feeling hopeful. Yet days later, rejection letters would arrive, one after another. Week after week, the same pattern unfolded. One particular day, I arrived at a law firm in the Sterick Building in downtown Memphis to take a typing and shorthand test. As I stepped into the lobby, I was struck by its elegance. A stunning vase of fresh flowers stood prominently in the entryway, and the entire office was adorned with rich mahogany wood, exuding an air of prestige. A young woman at the front desk greeted me and asked how she could assist.

I smiled politely and said, "I am here to take the test for the secretarial position."

She nodded and led me to another room where four other women were waiting. All of them were White. Soon after, we were escorted into a testing room equipped with five executive typewriters. The examiner began the test, starting with forty-five words per minute. As we progressed to sixty words per minute, only one other candidate managed to keep up. Then, she raised the bar to eighty words per minute. This time, I was the only one to successfully complete the test. I felt certain I could have gone even higher because I knew my skills allowed me to type up to 110 words per minute with ease. My confidence soared, and I was sure I had secured the position. However, the following week, I received a letter informing me that they had chosen someone else. That moment crushed me. I felt utterly defeated.

It was disheartening to realize that many doors seemed firmly shut, leaving me to question how to move forward. I became convinced that my race was the reason I was not being hired. It became painfully clear that things would never change unless I left Memphis, so that day, I resolved to leave. I didn't know how or when, but I promised myself that one day, I would get out of that city for good.

In that moment, I felt the steadfast resolve my mama demonstrated when she vowed never to return to Mississippi, no matter what life threw at her. That same strength became my anchor as I navigated my own hardships. I knew I had to leave Memphis, but I felt utterly trapped. I was a mother with a young child, no money, and no clear path forward. I felt overwhelmed by depression. I knew I needed to reevaluate everything and find a way to reclaim control over my future.

One evening at the hospital, Dr. Chauncey Daugherty, the Chairman of the Bluff City Medical Society, stopped by my office at Collins Chapel. The Society, made up of all the Black physicians in Memphis, was a big deal in the community. I shared my disappointment with my job search.

"All I'm looking for right now is a secretary position," I shared. "After typing eighty words per minute with no errors and taking a hundred words per minute shorthand, you would think I wouldn't have any problem finding a job."

He nodded in agreement.

"But in this prejudiced city, it *is* a problem," I said.

Dr. Daugherty smiled warmly and said, "Well, it just so happens that the board of governors is in need of a secretary."

He explained that they had received a grant from the Department of Health and Human Services to build a medical center in Memphis.

"We have put together a community board for the project, made up of doctors, activists, and notable Black leaders like Rev. James Lawson, and we need a secretary," he said.

Thrilled to hear this, I asked, "Is it a full-time position?"

"Indeed, it is, young lady," he said.

And right there, he offered me the opportunity to apply for the position of secretary to the board of governors for the Memphis Health Center. However, he made it clear to me that Ms. Lois Lyons, the director, would have to approve the application. Grateful and without hesitation, I accepted the opportunity, feeling no need for further questions. Dr. Daugherty then asked me to visit the office on Union Boulevard the following day to meet Ms. Lyons.

I arrived the next day at a cozy little office next door to the Commercial Appeal Newspaper Office. It featured three closed offices and an open area resembling a classroom. Ms. Lyons was a strikingly beautiful, petite Black woman with an unmistakable air of confidence. Despite her poised demeanor, she exuded warmth. Our conversation flowed easily, and she seemed genuinely impressed by my skills. She even mentioned how much she enjoyed the interview. Afterward, Ms. Lyons asked her secretary, Gerrelynn Fisher, to administer a typing test. I passed without issue, and to my surprise, Ms. Lyons offered me the job on the spot with a wage of $2.25 per hour. I was stunned by the offer, given that I was making only $1.33 per hour at Collins Chapel. This was a big raise, and it was full-time.

Excited, I drove home to share the news with my parents. When I told them about my new position, they were overjoyed. In their eyes, I had made it big time, especially since teachers in our neighborhood did not earn that kind of pay back then.

The frustration of my earlier job search had finally come to an end, and I felt immense gratitude toward Dr. Daugherty for helping make it possible. This experience taught me an important lesson: Never hesitate to share your situation with people in your network. I had no idea the position was available, but by openly communicating with the doctors I knew, an incredible opportunity was presented to me. It reinforced my belief in unity and connection.

I was thrilled to start my new job. My role included attending board meetings, taking shorthand minutes, and preparing meeting agendas. The position brought new responsibilities and opportunities, and though it was only a small step forward, it reignited my dreams. The unwavering support from the Black community, who recognized and appreciated the value of my abilities, was invaluable to me during this difficult time. When others failed to see my potential, they offered me an opportunity that changed everything, and I was overjoyed and deeply grateful to finally have a chance to prove myself. This fresh start reaffirmed my belief in the strength and resilience of our community. This opportunity was a lifeline that helped rebuild my confidence and allowed me to dream boldly again.

While working with the board of directors, I had the chance to accompany two board members to a conference in San Francisco. Having never been to California, I was beyond excited. One of the board members mentioned she had family in Los Angeles and planned to visit them before heading to San Francisco. She kindly invited me to join her, and I eagerly accepted. The thought of traveling to California felt like a dream come true. When we arrived in Los Angeles, I was awestruck. The city was stunning. Towering palm trees, rolling hills, and majestic mountains surrounded us. Everything looked vibrant and full of life. During our stay, we dined at amazing restaurants and even toured celebrity homes. The experience was surreal.

One of the highlights was visiting the iconic Santa Monica Pier, where the bright Ferris wheel and the sound of waves crashing against the shore created a magical atmosphere. We strolled along the bustling boardwalk, indulging in delicious ice cream and taking in street performances. We hiked to the Griffith Observatory and enjoyed the breathtaking panoramic views of the city skyline and the famous Hollywood sign. Los Angeles felt like a city of endless opportunities, where every corner revealed something new and exciting to explore.

After an unforgettable time in Los Angeles, we continued to San Francisco for the conference. San Francisco was an entirely different kind of beauty. Its iconic Golden Gate Bridge, steep streets, and historic cable cars created a charm that was both dynamic and timeless. The city buzzed with energy, and I felt invigorated. During the evenings, the board members and I explored the city together, solidifying our bond. We visited landmarks like Fisherman's Wharf and Lombard Street, soaking up everything San Francisco had to offer. For a young woman like me, stepping out of Memphis and experiencing a world so different was profoundly inspiring. It expanded my perspective and made me realize how much more there was to see, learn, and achieve.

That trip to California ignited within me a determination to dream bigger and work even harder. It was a travel experience that fundamentally shaped how I saw the possibilities of my future. As my time in California came to an end, I made a silent promise to myself to return one day. I didn't know when or how, but I felt certain that I was destined to make California my home. I returned to Memphis with a fire in my heart, ready to dedicate myself to making a difference, both for myself and for the community I cherished.

Adrian was about eight months old when I moved into my first apartment in Memphis. Located in the Beltz Apartments, our place was a modest two-bedroom unit that I was proud to call my own. Daddy ensured that I had everything I needed to make it comfortable and functional. He meticulously helped pick out furniture and household essentials, giving the space a warm and welcoming feel. Adrian and I moved into our new apartment and enjoyed life. We lived next door to Gerrelynn, who had worked with me at the Health Center. She had a son, Theta, the same age as Adrian. We enjoyed raising our boys and working together.

When Adrian turned two, we took a trip to New York City to visit my Aunt Jean, Mama's sister. Aunt Jean was an incredible woman with a strong and compassionate spirit. She was married to Uncle Jessie, and their family dynamic was both lively and full of love. During our visit, she introduced me to her brother-in-law, Ernest, Uncle Jessie's brother. Ernest and I quickly became friends, and he mentioned that he was considering moving back to the South. Aunt Jean had suggested Memphis as an option. When Ernest made the move to Memphis later that year, we began dating. He was a kind, hardworking man with a stable career as a welder at International Harvester, a well-respected and well-paying job for a Black man in Memphis at the time. My mother adored him and often praised his admirable qualities and secure profession. Yet, despite everything in his favor, I knew deep down that I was not in love with him.

Life as a single mother with a full-time job was demanding, but I was fortunate to have the unwavering support of my parents. Mama and Daddy were remarkable grandparents, stepping in to help me raise Adrian in ways I will always cherish. Their help lightened my load, but even with their support, I often felt stuck in Memphis, unable to escape the life I was living. The frustration and sense of stagnation weighed heavily on me, and Mama, always attuned to my emotions, noticed my struggle.

She thought Ernest was the answer to all my problems. To her, he was a good man who could bring stability and happiness into my life. She was sure he'd be a great father to Adrian and that I deserved the kind of love and support only a devoted husband could offer, the kind of love my daddy had always given her. Mama would not let up about it. She pushed me constantly to think about marrying Ernest, even using guilt when I hesitated. She'd say I was being selfish, not thinking about what was best for my son.

One warm June evening, Mama and I stood in her tiny kitchen, the smell of fresh cornbread still hanging in the air. Mama was at the counter, dredging chicken in flour, while I sat at the table watching Adrian play with wooden blocks on the floor at her feet. Suddenly, her words came sharply and unyielding.

"You think you are doing Adrian any favors living like this?" She turned to look at me, her flour-covered hands on her hips. "Ernest is a good man, steady, kind, and he loves you. What more could you want?"

Her words stung, but the look in her eyes really got to me. She was obviously disappointed, and my hesitation to marry Ernest seemed a betrayal, a failure to her and to Adrian. And she didn't stop there. She started talking about her own sacrifices, how she made choices for the family, not for herself.

"You are being selfish," she said, her voice softer now but still full of conviction. "You are only thinking about yourself, not Adrian. Don't you want him to have the life you had?"

Her disappointment hung in the air, thick and heavy, making me doubt myself. Mama had a way of turning her wishes into moral high ground, dressing them up in logic and love until they felt impossible to argue against. In that moment, I felt stuck, caught between my need to escape Memphis to live my dreams and the nagging fear that maybe she was right. Her words left me confused and emotionally drained. I didn't know what to do. Marrying Ernest seemed like the practical choice. He cared for me, he was financially secure, and he could offer Adrian the stability of a father figure.

While my heart wasn't certain, my mind told me I might not have a better option. I felt defeated. If I could not escape Memphis, maybe I could at least make the best of my circumstances. So, I asked myself: *Why not? Why not marry a man who loves me and can provide a better life for both me and my son? Why not try to find a little security in the midst of the chaos?*

I later realized I'd been asking the wrong questions. What I felt wasn't uncertainty about love—it was dissatisfaction with how my ambition and dreams were being sidelined. I didn't want to marry someone just to be cared for; I wanted a career more than a marriage. I aspired to become a president, to lead successfully, and those goals ran deep. I should have asked whether this path truly aligned with my future. Yet, despite that misjudgment, I conceded and chose to marry Ernest.

As our wedding approached, Ernest and I bought a house just a short walk from Mama and Daddy's, to stay connected to family. Our new home on Bridgeport Street in Memphis felt like a fresh start, full of possibilities. The house was modest but cozy, with a backyard that quickly became my favorite spot. At the center of the yard stood a magnificent magnolia tree, its branches stretching wide, offering shade and beauty. The house and the wedding both felt like the logical choice, but at the same time they felt like two of the biggest mistakes of my life.

Adrian was three years old when Ernest and I got married in the backyard of our new home. For the wedding, we set up an arch beneath the magnolia tree, adorned with vibrant flowers arranged lovingly by Mama and my sister, Charlett. More than thirty people gathered to celebrate with us, their laughter and conversation filling the air. We had prepared a feast for everyone, and the long tables were covered with delicious food that reflected our family's hospitality. Ernest beamed with joy throughout the day, thrilled to marry me and to step into his role as a father to Adrian. His excitement was evident in every word and gesture, and despite the uncertainties I felt, his happiness made the day undeniably special.

Moments before I stepped outside with my brother Jerome, who was to officiate the wedding, and my sister, Charlett, who was my matron of honor, my doubts overwhelmed me. I pulled Jerome and Charlett into the house and led them to the back bedroom, my heart pounding in my chest.

"I don't want to get married," I confessed, my voice trembling.

Jerome's expression remained calm, though his jaw tightened. "Don't you think you should have figured that out before now?" he asked, his tone steady but pointed.

Charlett's eyes widened in disbelief. "What the hell are you going to do now?" she blurted, her voice rising in panic.

Tears streamed down my face as the weight of confusion and fear bore down on me. I sank onto the edge of the bed, clutching my head, unable to make sense of the storm raging inside me. I covered my face with both hands, then stood up.

"I don't know what to do! I am so confused," I screamed, looking at my sister and brother. "Mama wants me to get married, but I don't know what to do!"

I stood there for a minute, looking in the mirror. Then, in an instant, I turned around and looked at Jerome and shouted, "Let's go."

Charlett asked, "Where are we going?"

I didn't answer. I grabbed her hand and pulled her out of the house along with me. At that point, there was no turning back. They followed me outside. My siblings stood there shocked at my sudden and certain change of mind. They could not have known the torment I felt at that moment, but they would certainly have understood the devotion and commitment that guided me.

The truth was undeniable: I didn't want to marry Ernest. Not really. The thought of standing beside him, committing myself to a life I knew deep down wasn't right, felt suffocating. But Mama had poured her heart into the wedding. It was her dream, her vision of a perfect life where her children were settled and contented. She had devoted so much time, energy, and pride to orchestrating the day. The idea of shattering that dream, of disappointing her after all she had invested in, felt unbearable. Her happiness weighed on me like a heavy shroud, smothering my own desires until they seemed selfish and insignificant. In those agonizing moments, as the clock ticked closer to the ceremony, I searched desperately for a way out. I longed for some miraculous solution that would free me from my choice without hurting anyone. But I found nothing. My fear of letting Mama down outweighed my own need to honor the truth within me.

Jerome officiated the ceremony as planned. I smiled and played the part, pretending to be happy, even as my heart felt heavy with the weight of a shattered dream. The dream of escaping Memphis, of starting a new life, was gone. I told myself I was doing the right thing for Mama, who was happy to see me married to a good man and providing a father figure for my son. But inside, I felt my spirit crumbling under the weight of disappointment. On that day, I buried my own desires to meet their expectations, trading my happiness for the fragile illusion of peace.

After the wedding, I pretended to be happy. On the surface, my life looked perfect. I was married to a kind man with a stable job.

I taught Sunday school at Alice Avenue Church of Christ, worked a prestigious secretarial position for the Bluff City Medical Society, and drove a Lincoln New Yorker. I lived in a beautiful home, and Mama was so proud of the life I had built. But none of it brought me joy. While Mama celebrated what she saw as my success, I was drowning in misery. For a year, I kept up the act. I smiled through my marriage, smiled at work, and smiled in church, trying to maintain the illusion of a happy life. But eventually, the cracks began to show. My unhappiness seeped out of every corner of my life: at home, at work, and even in my faith. I felt trapped, suffocating under the weight of unfulfilled dreams and living a life that did not feel like my own. I began to ask myself if there was a way out. *Can I escape without hurting anyone? What sacrifices will I have to make?*

The guilt was unbearable. I chastised myself for being selfish, for daring to think about my own happiness when my current life seemed to bring so much joy to others, especially Mama. But the suffocation was relentless, and I knew deep down that something had to change. I had sacrificed my dreams to fulfill my mother's aspirations. I understood that she only wanted the best for Adrian and me. Mama believed that a traditional wife's role was ideal for me, but I knew it wasn't the life I wanted. I had bigger dreams, a vision for my future that extended far beyond the confines of Memphis. I finally confessed to myself that marrying Ernest had been a mistake and the life I was living was too small for my ambitions.

Frustrated and desperate for a way out, I began researching opportunities with the military. My good friend Frazier had joined the Navy to escape Memphis, and his experience gave me hope. Frazier, like me, was twenty-four years old and had a son, yet he had taken a bold step to change his situation. One day, I attended a meeting for the health center in downtown Memphis. Among the attendees was an impressive Black Navy master chief, a distinguished man in charge of Mid-South recruiting programs for the Navy. He was a personal friend of one of the doctors and stood out in his Navy uniform, which was adorned with stripes and medals. At first glance, I thought he might have been a general, but one thing was clear, he carried an air of authority. Determined to speak with him, I made it a point to sit at his table along with other board members, using my position as secretary to the board of directors as an entry point.

I introduced myself and struck up a conversation about the military, asking him questions about the roles of women and minorities in the armed forces. His responses were straightforward, honest, and insightful. He didn't sugarcoat the challenges, but he also emphasized the opportunities. He shared some of his own accomplishments, and I could tell he was the real deal.

As we talked, I opened up about my struggles in Memphis and my educational background. He explained that many women had found success in the military, particularly in the Navy and Air Force. His words resonated with me, sparking a new sense of possibility. Inspired by our conversation, I became determined to explore this path further, envisioning a future where I could chart my own course and leave behind the limitations of my current life.

Driving home, I couldn't shake the thought that joining the military might be my escape. Being married with a child added layers of complexity. Ernest would have to give his consent for me to enlist. My mind raced as I tried to figure out how I could convince him to sign the papers, and what arrangements I would make for Adrian. Despite the obstacles, I was determined to find a way. Somehow, this was going to be my way out.

A few days later, I called the Navy master chief, and we scheduled the aptitude test, which I passed. After reviewing my results, he recommended that I start as an airman, explaining that the ideal role for me would not be available until later in the year. He assured me that before I completed boot camp, he would make sure I would be assigned to cryptology school.

On the drive home, I realized I had my work cut out for me with Ernest. This was not only about leaving Memphis, it was about leaving him too. But I couldn't let him know that. If he knew, there was no way he'd sign the papers. So, I decided to plan a special night to ease into the conversation. I asked Mama if she could watch Adrian for the night so Ernest and I could have a date night. She didn't mind at all because she loved having Adrian over. We all call him "Slug," by the way. Daddy gave him that nickname when he was little because, instead of walking or crawling properly, he'd drag himself around the floor super slow, using one hand, like a little slug. He didn't start walking until he was fifteen months, not because there was anything wrong with him, but because he figured being carried was easier. So, Slug became his nickname.

After dropping Adrian off at Mama's, I rushed back home to cook Ernest's favorite meal: fried chicken, creamed corn, collard greens, cornbread, and my special banana pudding. When Ernest walked in and saw the spread, he said, "What did I do to deserve this meal?" He kissed me, then headed straight to the bedroom to take his usual post-work shower. Meanwhile, I kept busy in the kitchen, running through how I would start the conversation. I had a plan: dinner, a nice conversation, and a sexy, fun night to seal the deal. We sat down to eat and talked about work, church, and even tossed around ideas for a vacation to New Orleans. Afterward, we moved to the living room, and I decided it was time.

I leaned in and said softly, "So, the Navy has this special program for women. If I do it, I could really build my computer skills."

Ernest raised an eyebrow. "Where's this program?"

"It's in Millington, at the Naval base," I said.

"Do you have to quit your job, or can you keep it while you train?" he asked.

I took a breath.

"It's a little more complicated than that. I would have to join the Navy for two years, but I would still be stationed in Memphis. It would basically be like having a regular job."

That was the first lie.

"I would be training as an air traffic controller," I added. Then, came the second lie. I continued to explain that after boot camp, I would be stationed at Millington, right outside Memphis.

"It would be only ten weeks of training in Orlando, and during that time, Mama could take care of Adrian," I said, trying to make it sound easy, doable. But inside, I knew this was not simple at all, it was a bunch of lies.

Ernest hesitated, looking unsure.

"Martha, I don't know about this. What if a war breaks out? Will they send you to fight?"

I smiled, trying to ease his mind. "No, they don't send women to fight. We do desk jobs. It's nothing dangerous."

He didn't look entirely convinced, but I leaned in and gave him a big kiss, then pulled him toward the bedroom. We had a romantic night, and for a little while, it felt like everything was fine. Afterward, I looked at him and said, "Ernest, can I go?"

He sighed, running a hand through his hair. "I don't know about this whole 'ten weeks away' thing. That's a long time, Martha."

"You'll be okay, I promise," I said softly, sitting up in bed. I grabbed the form I had stashed on the nightstand and handed it to him. "I need you to sign this so I can go."

I knew I had to act fast. If he had the chance to talk to anyone, my mama, the church deacons, anyone, they'd convince him not to let me go. I couldn't risk that. He stared at the paper for a moment, then looked back at me. "You are really sure about this?"

"I am," I said, nodding. "It's something I need to do."

He hesitated, but eventually, he grabbed a pen and signed it. Relief flooded through me as I threw my arms around him, giving him a huge hug. "Thank you," I whispered, holding onto him tightly. *Mission accomplished.*

That night, as Ernest drifted off to sleep, I slipped into the other room. I couldn't help myself: I started prancing around in excitement, my heart racing at the thought of finally escaping. I was going to leave, to start over. To join the Navy and find something new. But as the excitement bubbled up, so did a pang of guilt. Ernest was a good man. He didn't deserve this deceitfulness. I knew he was not happy either, not fully, but he kept holding on to hope that one day I would love him the way he loved me. And deep down, I knew I could not. I stopped prancing and stood there in the quiet, staring at the form he had signed. I felt torn with emotions of both guilt and excitement swirling together. But I knew one thing for sure: I could not keep pretending. I needed to leave, and now, I had my way out.

The key lesson here is to never abandon your dreams in favor of someone else's vision for your life. Seeking advice is valuable; it's part of the Unity in my G.U.T.S. framework. Whether advice is solicited or freely given, you must thoughtfully evaluate it. Decide what aligns with your goals. Accept all, part, or none of it, but always remember, the final decision is yours. Never feel guilty for declining advice that doesn't serve your dreams. The greatest mistake you can make in pursuing your dreams is letting others dictate your success or allowing their influence to override your desires and plans.

Success is deeply personal, and when you make your own decisions, you can face the outcomes—good or bad—with greater resilience. I have found it far easier to forgive myself for my own missteps than to live with bad decisions made under someone else's influence.

Advice can be a powerful tool, but it's just that, a tool. The responsibility of carving your path rests with you, and often, achieving your dreams will require sacrifices. Stay true to what you want and trust yourself to navigate the journey forward.

Lessons in G.U.T.S.

Living by G.U.T.S. is not always easy, but it's a path that brings clarity, resilience, and meaningful success. There was a time when I fell out of alignment with the principles of G.U.T.S., and those experiences taught me their true value. Straying from these core values brought setbacks that I had to overcome, but it also deepened my understanding of their importance. Stay grounded in gratitude, unity, trustworthiness, and spirituality, no matter the challenges you face.

G — Gratitude: I'm deeply grateful that my relationship with God led me to give birth to my son, Adrian. He has been a profound blessing, filling my life with a mother's love. I'm also grateful for my three grandsons, who have brought me even more love and joy. The job opportunity at Collins Chapel opened doors for me—advancing my career, restoring my hope, and providing financial stability. I'm thankful for the chance that encouraged me to step out and pursue my dream.

I'm grateful that Ernest signed for me to go into the Navy. Although I'm not proud of how it happened, I'm thankful I didn't prolong his pain by staying in a marriage where there was respect but not love. The lessons I learned were a blessing: deception should never be used—honesty, even when it hurts, is the best path to fulfilling your purpose. I'm grateful for the turning points that set me on the right path. Be thankful for challenges; they are the steppingstones to your dreams and success. Every struggle shapes who you are and brings you closer to your goals.

U — Unity: I couldn't have progressed without the help of others—the Master Chief, my family doctor, my father, and many more who supported me as I moved toward my goals. Advice can be valuable, but it must align with your own desires, values, and plans. Stay true to yourself while considering the guidance of others.

T — Trustworthiness: Honesty really is the key to meaningful success. I learned that the hard way. There were times when I let desperation get the better of me, and I compromised my integrity. It left me feeling guilty and it caused me to hurt the people I cared about. Sure, being dishonest might give you quick results, but it never leads to real happiness or fulfillment. I'll be honest, dealing with the fallout from those lies was rough. It caused so much pain, arguments and anger with my mom, years of unforgiveness between Ernest and me, and some awful moments overall. Looking back, that drama could have been avoided if I had been honest from the start. I wasn't true to myself, especially when I married Ernest, and that decision was built on a lie which only led to more lies and heartache. The biggest lesson I took from all of this is to always be truthful with yourself and in every situation you face. It saves so much pain overall.

S — Spirituality: Too often, we act without even stopping to seek God's guidance. It's like we just go ahead with our plans and only turn to Him afterward, asking for forgiveness. I've been there. During this season in my life when everything felt so out of control, I was disappointed—disappointed in the church, in my marriage, in my life, in my career, and in the way things were unfolding. And honestly, that disappointment led me to drift away from God. I wasn't asking God what to do. I was just making my own plans, thinking I could figure it out on my own. But looking back, I realize how important it is to consult Him first, before taking steps that might lead us away from His will.

There were moments in my journey when my actions didn't align with His plans. But that's why it's so crucial to stay connected to Him. When we maintain that relationship, He has a way of putting us back on track. God orders our steps before we even take them. I can just imagine Him looking at me during those troubling times, shaking His head with a little smile, saying, "What is she doing now? Let me show her some mercy and guide her back." That's the kind of God I serve— one who already knows where He's taking me and lovingly redirects me when I stray.

CHAPTER 6

Running Away to Achieve the Dream

Sometimes, when you decide to achieve something that is not easy, you have to do it and not be afraid.

I arrived by bus at the Orlando Naval Training Center for boot camp in March 1976. As I sat in the office, I took in my surroundings. There were more than two-hundred women from all corners of the United States gathered to begin a new chapter of our lives. Some huddled with friends from their hometowns, while others, like me, sat quietly, taking it all in. The room buzzed with a mix of excitement and nervous energy.

When they called my name, they told me I was assigned to Company 3055D and pointed me toward the sign marking our area. My first thought was *Why the 'D'?* None of the other companies seemed to have a letter tacked on.

I followed the other women onto another bus, which took us to our new quarters on base. That's where we met Petty Officer Griffin. She was short, blonde, White, with a round face and broad shoulders, definitely someone who looked like she meant business. She was our company's basic training commander.

We stood in formation outside our quarters as she greeted us. Her tone was calm but firm, with this measured politeness that made it clear she was in charge.

"You'll be here as long as you need to be," she said. "For most, it's nine weeks. For some, it's as long as seventeen weeks." Then she added, "You've been selected as a Drill Team. That's why you're called Company 3055D. As a drill team, you'll perform during the last three weeks of your stay at the graduation ceremonies. The first six weeks will be spent training for that performance."

I wasn't sure if this was a good thing or a bad thing. But I figured being on a drill team might come with some special privileges, and anything "special" had to be good, right? Still, my mind kept circling back to one thing she said: *seventeen weeks.* My immediate reaction was disbelief. *There is no way I will stay here for seventeen weeks.*

Petty Officer Griffin directed us to enter the barracks that would serve as our home for the next few weeks. She then began walking through the room, stopping to speak with recruits one by one. She asked each woman why she'd joined the Navy and what specialty she planned to pursue. As the questioning continued, I grew increasingly anxious, unable to shake thoughts of what might prolong my time there. When Griffin turned her gaze toward me, I forced a smile, but my heart was pounding.

"Stand up," she commanded. I shot to my feet as she approached. Her eyes studied me intently. "Why are you here?" she asked.

Her question felt heavier than it sounded. Out of sixty-five women in the company, only five of us were Black. I could sense that she genuinely wanted to know my story, but I could not bring myself to tell the truth, that I was running away from home, escaping Memphis, the discrimination, and a life full of setbacks. Instead, I replied that I had enlisted to pursue a career as a cryptologist.

Before I could even finish, she glanced at her roster and interrupted, "No, you are an airman set for air traffic control training."

I hesitated, then replied, "Yes, that's what I was told, but my recruiter assured me I would be reassigned to cryptology during boot camp."

Griffin laughed loudly. Shaking her head, she said, "In my eight years of training recruits, I have never seen anyone have their specialty changed in boot camp, and I doubt the Navy is going to make you an exception." Her tone carried a mix of amusement and disbelief as she muttered, "The things these recruiters will say to get women to join these days!" Still laughing, she looked directly at me and said, "They lied to you."

Her words landed like a punch to my gut. My face burned with humiliation, and I felt a surge of betrayal toward the Master Chief who had promised me something that now seemed impossible. Griffin continued, her voice tinged with mockery. "Don't get your hopes up. You'll leave boot camp as an airman, not a cryptologist." She walked away, still chuckling, glancing back at me as if amused by my naivete.

As I sank back into my seat, tears threatened to spill, and I quickly wiped them away. I didn't want anyone to see me crying. My heart raced, my chest tightened with anxiety, and my mind replayed her words again and again. *They lied to you.*

Before I could fully process my emotions, a voice boomed, "Attention on deck!" Instinctively, I shot to my feet, standing at attention. But my thoughts were elsewhere, tangled in confusion and disappointment. The rest of the evening passed in a blur as we were assigned bunk beds and given instructions. I went through the motions, but my mind was stuck, reeling from the realization that my journey in the Navy was already shaping up to be different from what I had imagined.

In that moment, I knew I had to do everything in my power to make the best of the situation. That night, as I tossed and turned in bed, I couldn't shake the image of Griffin laughing. *Is this really happening?* If I became an airman, my training would take place in Memphis, and I had to rethink my plan of action to prepare for that reality. As I rolled over to try to sleep, I made up my mind: I would hold onto hope. I prayed to God, asking for strength because I couldn't bear for my dreams to be shattered again.

The next morning, Petty Officer Griffin announced that she needed to select ten boot camp officers for the company. I was determined to secure a leadership position. When she revealed the organizational chart, I set my sights on one of the top four roles. The room buzzed with the energy of so many women in one place, but it became clear that we would need to work together; after all, that was the essence of boot camp.

At twenty-four, I was one of the oldest recruits, with only one woman older than me at twenty-nine. The rest were between eighteen and twenty-one. Although I had never called cadence before, I was a former cheerleader with a strong, commanding voice. I remembered hearing cadence during high school drill team practices, so when Griffin asked if anyone could step up to call cadence, I immediately volunteered. For the next two days, she asked me to lead cadence whenever we marched out of the facilities. When the officer roles were announced, I was thrilled to be named the 2nd platoon leader, responsible for thirty-two women. My duties included calling cadence as we marched across campus and giving orders to my peers, a welcome change from simply following orders. Being in a leadership position during boot camp was a privilege, and I was proud to have earned it.

I have always believed in taking bold steps toward my goals, and I have never been afraid of a challenge. When I learned that being a recruit officer would put me in a better position than a regular soldier, with added responsibilities and benefits, I jumped at the chance. Instead of waiting to see how selection would unfold or relying on unknown criteria, I seized the opportunity to volunteer. Being in that position made boot camp a little easier. I was not doing all the work; I was supervising it. Early on, I realized it was better for me to be giving orders than taking them, especially since I had a lot more life experience than the seventeen- and eighteen-year-old girls around me.

By the eighth week of boot camp, we were finally nearing the finish line. This was the week we would receive our assignments. Petty Officer Griffin entered the barracks, a stack of papers in hand.

"Okay, sailors, gather around," she said. "It's time to receive your orders."

For the past seven weeks, I had tried not to dwell on what she had told me when I first arrived, that she had never seen a recruit's orders change. Now, as the moment of truth approached, I braced for the possibility that she might be wrong. If she was not, I would be headed back to Memphis, a fate I desperately wanted to avoid. If she was wrong, it would confirm that joining the Navy had been the right decision and that the master chief, who had promised to help me, had both power and integrity.

As Petty Officer Griffin began calling out names and handing out orders, anxiety gnawed at me. My last name started with U, which meant I would be among the last called. The waiting was agonizing. My heart raced as I silently prayed, begging the Lord not to send me back to Memphis. Around me, other girls squealed with excitement as their orders matched their hopes, their joy heightening my own apprehension. My thoughts spiraled as Griffin got closer to my name, now handing out orders to recruits whose last names began with S.

Finally, she called my name. I stood, my entire body trembling, hands shaking as I faced her, simultaneously afraid and hopeful for what would come next. As she extended her hand and we shook, she looked at me with an expression of both surprise and warmth.

"I don't know who you know," she said, "but this is the first time I've ever seen this. You are going to Cryptology A School in Pensacola, Florida."

I gasped, then screamed, "Oh my God!"

She smiled broadly and said, "You deserve it."

In that moment, I felt seen. Perhaps she had recognized my leadership during our grueling weeks of training, which led my team to excel in inspections as we followed every rule. The excitement was indescribable.

My dream had come true. At last, I could begin practicing the computer training I had always desired. But most importantly, I had escaped Memphis. My life was finally about to change. I didn't know exactly what lay ahead, but I was certain of one thing: It would not be in Memphis.

After graduating from boot camp, I returned to Memphis for a week before heading to Cryptology A School in Pensacola. Seeing Adrian again filled me with joy. I had missed him so much during my time in Orlando. But when I reunited with Ernest, his expression was heavy with sadness.

"I know this is over," he said. "I knew you weren't coming back." Then, with a pained voice, he added, "Please don't play with my emotions. If you're leaving, just tell me. I don't want to hold onto the house or anything."

At first, I didn't know how to respond, but eventually, I told him the truth. "It's not going to work," I said. "I want more out of life than what Memphis can offer. I've finally escaped, and now I have a chance to live my dreams."

Ernest was deeply disappointed, but he accepted my decision. I told him to keep the house; I only wanted to take my clothes. I didn't need anything except my freedom. Letting go of my old life was not easy, but it was necessary. Leaving Memphis was a physical move and a step toward the life I had always envisioned for myself.

My mom didn't understand my decision. She was still upset with me for joining the Navy. Anytime I asked her for anything that did not involve me moving back home to Memphis, she'd get angry. So, when I asked her to watch Adrian for another three months while I went to school in Pensacola, she tried to guilt-trip me about leaving him. I didn't want to get an apartment for such a short time, but every conversation with her felt like it was meant to make me feel bad about leaving Adrian and Ernest. I was already sad about leaving Adrian, and the constant guilt made it harder.

The funny thing is, Mama and Daddy were always happy to have Adrian with them because he brought so much joy to their lives.

But Mama continued to push me to change my plans, come back to Memphis, and be with Ernest. She wanted me to settle down and have a stable life. She couldn't see how that was going to happen with me being in the military and so far away from them. Even though it was hard, I reminded myself that once I got my final orders, I would have Adrian with me again. So, I tried to let some of Mama's behavior slide because, in the end, I knew she only wanted what she thought was best for me.

Arriving in Pensacola felt like entering a new world. The warm air and lively campus were a sharp contrast to boot camp's intensity. Cryptology A School offered a fresh start and a chance to prove myself. The rigorous courses pushed my mental limits, rivaling the physical challenges of boot camp. Surrounded by people mastering skills I had dreamed of, I thrived in the intense training in codes, ciphers, and analysis. The challenge energized me, and each new lesson boosted my confidence. Long study nights and the pressure to excel tested me, but I loved every moment, knowing I was on the right path.

After completing A School, I was stationed in Winter Harbor, Maine, within Acadia National Forest—far from my dream destinations like Edzell, Scotland, or San Diego. The small base housed about 250 Navy personnel, mostly married, and felt remote and quiet, nothing like the adventurous life I had imagined. Instead of traveling the world, I found myself confronting personal challenges, including the decision to divorce Ernest. Despite my family's attachment to him and their hope for our reconciliation, I knew I had to move forward. I had planned to get an apartment so I could bring Adrian to live with me after Christmas. I was ready to close that chapter of my life.

Within my first month, Ronald Scharf, a young Navy reservist, arrived for a two-week duty. While many single men on base showed interest in me, I kept my personal life private. Ron, however, stood out. We rode the bus together to the communication center, and his interest was clear. At first, I wasn't sure of his background; his red cornrows and light complexion reminded me of my brother Vance.

One day, Ron asked if it would matter to me if he was White. I looked at him and confidently said, "No, you're not." He tried to mix things up, mentioning his mother was Hispanic and his father White, as if that would change anything, but it didn't matter. Ron was charming, attractive, and I enjoyed his company. I found myself no longer caring about the details of his ethnicity. Over the course of his two weeks stay in September, we spent a lot of time together and grew close. I was encouraged by two things: 1) he was single, and 2) he lived in California. That made all the difference. Before he left, he asked if we could continue talking after he returned home, and of course, I said, yes. We talked three to four times a week. Even though it was long distance, we continued to talk and I began to like him even more.

About a month after Ron returned to California, I became gravely ill. My menstrual cycle seemed endless, leaving me in constant pain and unable to work. Some days, the cramps were so excruciating that I had to be rushed to the emergency room for relief. My weight plummeted from 118 pounds to 100, alarming the base physician, who quickly referred me to a local OB/GYN specialist. Despite numerous tests, the specialist could not pinpoint the cause of my illness. His only recommendation was a hysterectomy, which I firmly refused.

Both the base priest and the doctor advised me to consider leaving the Navy. They suggested I return to Memphis and offered the option of an honorable discharge due to my medical condition. But going back wasn't an option for me. I had worked so hard to escape my past, and returning felt like surrendering. I didn't share my illness with my family because I didn't want them to worry, nor did I want them to see me as defeated. So, I chose to stay, hoping against hope that my condition would improve. Unfortunately, it did not; it only worsened. Still, I refused to let the illness define my future.

One morning early in December, my supervisor, Chief Cousins, called me into his office. Chief was a White guy, about five foot, ten inches tall, with a kind heart. He'd been in the Navy for twenty-eight years and was ready to retire. He was a heavy smoker, a great leader, and compassionate. Although he never said it outright, I knew he didn't fully believe women belonged in the military. Chief believed men and women had different roles, and his actions sometimes reflected a double standard. Under his command, men swabbed the deck (mopped the floors), took out the trash, and lifted the heavy stuff. The guys hated it, but Chief was in charge, and that's how it was. Even the base commander agreed with him.

Chief was from the area and loved telling stories about his hometown, Ellsworth, and nearby Winter Harbor, Maine. He had trained me in my job, even ensuring I earned my sharpshooter medal. Over the months, he became a father figure to me. During our frequent walks by the ocean during lunch breaks, he shared pieces of his life with me. I trusted and respected him deeply, and I believed he genuinely cared about me.

It was getting close to Christmas when he sat me down with a mix of concern and determination in his eyes.

"Martha," he said, "you shouldn't be in the Navy." He brought up things I had told him before, how I would join to get away from my life in Memphis. Then he said, gently but firmly, "You are sick, and you need to go home. The Navy is not ready for you, Martha. You have so much more to offer the world, and you'll never reach your full potential here."

He paused, taking a long drag of his Pall Mall non-filter cigarette, then continued, "Go home to your son. Get well. This place won't be good for you after I'm gone."

I broke down in tears. Chief reassured me that I would receive an honorable discharge and keep all my GI benefits. He encouraged me to return to college full-time, finish my degree, and pursue a different path, one where I wouldn't have to struggle through my recovery while trying to work. As I left his office, he gave me one parting piece of advice: "Martha, take the discharge and go home. This is not the place for you anymore."

I drove to the chapel and spoke to the chaplain about my situation and the Chief's conversation with me. He already knew of my illness, and we had been praying for me to get well. He looked at me with sadness and said, "I agree with the Chief; you should go home." As I cried, he prayed for me.

That evening, I called Ron. I explained the situation and asked if I could come to California and stay with him while I got back on my feet. I made it clear that I would be bringing my son, Adrian, with me. "Yes, yes," he said excitedly. "Please come." Ron was thrilled. He knew I had already filed for divorce, and I think he saw this as a chance to build a more permanent relationship with me. At the time, he was working as a truck driver for Pepsi-Cola, and he said he'd move into a family apartment to make room for us.

I received an honorable discharge from the military a few days before Christmas. Although I knew it was due to medical reasons, the paperwork simply stated, "Honorable Discharge." The moment was bittersweet, leaving me with a whirlwind of emotions that I struggled to process. Unsure of what to feel or think, I called Ron to let him know I was officially discharged and would soon be going home to pick up my son. He mentioned needing two weeks to prepare, which worked out perfectly since I also needed that time after leaving Winter Harbor.

Next, I called my mother to share the news. I told her I would be home for Christmas but planned to move to California in January. Her voice shot through the phone like an alarm.

"Have you lost your mind? What about Adrian? He's not going to California!" Then came the inevitable question I had been dreading: "What about Ernest, your husband?" I had not yet told her that I had filed for divorce, but it felt like the moment to come clean. Her response was swift; she hung up the phone.

My life felt like a tangled mess. Hurting Ernest and my mother had never been my intention, but looking back, I should have stood up for myself from the beginning. I didn't want to marry him, and if I had been honest about that, none of this would have happened. Instead, I ended up in a situation where I lied, deceived, and broke someone's heart to undo a mistake that never should have occurred. All my choices and my actions left me overwhelmed with sadness. I decided I would return to Memphis, pick up Adrian, and leave quietly. If only I could turn back time, I would rewrite everything. My mother was furious, but my daddy reassured me that, in time, things would work out. Somehow, I had to believe he was right.

I purchased my airline ticket, sold my car, and flew home, not sure what to expect when I got there. Mama picked me up from the airport and we drove home with little conversation. I could tell she was upset, and I understood why, but I couldn't bring myself to initiate a conversation, so we rode in silence.

While I was in the service, Daddy had opened a soul food restaurant on McLemore across from the famous Stax Records studio in Memphis. Stax was a cornerstone of Memphis soul, known for its racially integrated studio and a string of hits for artists like Otis Redding, Isaac Hayes, and Booker T. & the M.G.'s. Sadly, the label ultimately closed due to financial difficulties. Daddy was told they'd reopen, so he went ahead and started the restaurant anyway.

As soon as I got home, I went to talk with him, the only one who understood me. I met Daddy at the restaurant, and as we sat down, he looked at me and said, "I don't know this guy, but if you say he's a good man, I trust your instincts."

His words brought me comfort, but as the weight of my emotions spilled over, I broke into tears. He pulled me into a tight embrace while I cried on his shoulder.

"Daddy," I said, "I cannot stay here."

He sighed deeply.

"I know," he replied, "but remember, you can always come back if things don't work out."

At the table, I picked up the phone and booked airline tickets for Adrian and me to head to Los Angeles at 10:00 the next morning.

Later that evening, Ernest stopped by the restaurant and asked if we could talk. We sat in his car, both of us crying as we talked.

"Martha, you've really hurt me," he said. "I moved here from New York thinking we'd have a long life together, with children and everything." His voice broke as he added, "But all we have is a house. And that doesn't mean anything to me because it's not a home."

I was crying too.

"Ernest, I'm so sorry," I said. But it felt like my words didn't reach him.

He looked at me and said, "I hope you find happiness. Your mother told me you're leaving for California tomorrow."

"Yes," I said quietly.

"Enjoy life," he said. I could hear it in his voice; he was done.

I knew it was time to go. I opened the door, turned back to him one last time, and said, "Ernest, I really am sorry." Then I closed the door and walked back into the restaurant, leaving him behind. That was the last time I saw him.

The next day, Daddy and Mama drove me to the airport. Mama cried the whole way there, big heavy sobs that made my heart ache. Adrian was emotional too, but he couldn't hide how excited he was to be going with me, especially since we'd be flying on an airplane.

At the airport, Daddy hugged me tightly.

"You know your way home, and the door is always open," he said.

Mama grabbed Adrian and hugged him, then turned to me, her face filled with anger.

"You're making a mistake," she said sharply. "You'll be back." But as she started to walk away, she stopped, turned around, and ran back to me. She pulled me into a hug and whispered, "I love you."

I broke down crying. "I love you too, Mama," I said through my tears.

Adrian and I boarded the plane, and as we found our seats, I was flooded with so many emotions. I was happy to have Adrian with me and excited to leave Memphis behind. But I was scared too. I didn't know what to expect, and the thought of being in California alone with no family felt overwhelming. Still, deep down, I knew this was the right decision, a fresh start in Southern California. I was leaving Memphis again, but this time it felt different. I didn't know what the future would hold, but I was ready to take the leap.

The path ahead was far from clear, but I clung to the belief that this fresh start could lead to something better. I didn't have all the answers, but one thing was certain: I had a new chance to chase my dreams and finally leave Memphis behind. I promised myself I wouldn't squander it. After all, the worst-case scenario was simply going back if things didn't work out. Fear wouldn't hold me back. This was my moment to try again, and I was determined to make the most of it.

Achieving my dream required profound sacrifices. I had made the difficult choice to leave my four-year-old son in my mother's care for over a year. My desire to build a life beyond the confines of segregation was so strong that I pursued every possible path to create opportunities for myself. When one door closed, I refused to accept no as the final answer. My resilience and determination pushed me forward, even in the face of seemingly insurmountable challenges. I knew there was always another way as long as I didn't give up. Joining the military was a pivotal decision that worked in my favor. Even when I faced personal health struggles, the military played a key role in my journey. Looking back, I see it as part of God's plan to lead me to California, a place that ultimately changed my life.

To achieve your dreams, you must start by understanding yourself. Take time to reflect on your habits, such as whether you tend to worry too much or give up easily, and identify what truly drives you. This self-awareness allows you to set realistic goals that align with your personality and aspirations. Recognizing your strengths is important, though identifying your weaknesses is even more crucial. These areas are where you can rely on your network for support, knowledge, and guidance. By deepening your self-awareness, you will also gain clarity on what success means to you, whether that's achieving financial stability, reaching a significant milestone, or coming back stronger after a setback.

Knowing who you are at your core is so important. Take the time to figure out what defines you and the values you stand for. When opportunities come your way, be ready to grab them. Achieving your dreams isn't easy; it takes confidence, determination, and a commitment to action. Be willing to sacrifice your time, resources, comfort, and even your sense of balance.

Imagine yourself chasing your biggest dream, and have that clear vision of what success looks like to you. This gives you direction and fuels your motivation to stay focused. But success doesn't arrive all at once; it unfolds in stages. Achieving your ultimate dream requires breaking it down into measurable milestones and timelines. These smaller victories will guide you toward your larger goal.

Let's be honest, fear often gets in the way. Fear of failure stops so many dreams before they even get started. Negative thoughts often come from overthinking or worrying about what could go wrong, creating a cycle of fear and self-doubt. To break this cycle, reframe your perspective. Getting over the fear of failure is easier when you break your goals into smaller, doable steps. Focusing on one thing at a time makes everything feel less overwhelming and more manageable. Every win boosts your confidence and keeps you moving forward so you can build momentum and see progress without stressing over mistakes. Celebrate small successes to stay motivated and be ready to take the next step.

You are capable and you are worthy of achieving your dreams, even if fear is tagging along for the ride. Keep moving forward. Trust that there is a bigger plan for you and believe in yourself to make it happen. Taking that leap, even with doubts, is always better than not trying at all. Believing in yourself tips the odds in your favor. When opportunity knocks, don't hesitate. Seize it. Don't let fear or self-doubt hold you back, especially when the door is already open for you to step through.

Understanding who you are and the depth of your desire is key to defining your success. Success is deeply personal; it's unique to you. Your values and your willingness to make the necessary sacrifices will serve as your compass, guiding you through your journey.

Lessons in G.U.T.S.

G — Grateful: I am deeply thankful to my parents for their steadfast support in caring for my son while I fulfilled my duties in the military. Their love and dedication gave me the strength to persevere. The moment I stopped pretending and fully embraced responsibility for my life and dreams was a turning point that changed everything. I am equally grateful to Ernest, whose unwavering love remained constant, even during times when I felt unworthy of it. And to Ron, I owe immense gratitude for welcoming my son and me with open arms, offering us a fresh start and a new chapter in California. Though my choices brought disappointment to my mother and Ernest, I chose not to carry guilt. While I regret causing them pain, I have learned to honor their feelings while continuing to move forward with purpose and hope.

U — Unity: Success is not a solitary achievement. Many people added their valuable input and offered much-needed support to help me when I needed it most. Some acted in unity, like my parents and Ernest, in making sure Adrian was cared for while I was away. Others, like my priest, my doctor, and my Chief, worked within a system to ensure my well-being was prioritized. Their unity gave me the courage to move forward.

T — Trustworthiness: The journey to resetting my soul began with a commitment to honesty, allowing me to move forward with a heart rooted in trust and integrity. I learned the importance of saying what

I mean and meaning what I say, as honesty consistently leads to better outcomes than dishonesty. Looking back, I should have told my mother and Ernest that I didn't want to get married. Instead, I went along with their plans, ignoring my own feelings. That lack of honesty set me back, hurt others, and unnecessarily complicated my life. Being truthful with yourself and others is always the better path as it brings peace of mind, reduces anxiety, and fosters self-acceptance. While challenges may still arise, facing them with honesty and inner calm leaves you far better equipped to handle them.

S — Spirituality: The path that brought me here is one I could never have orchestrated on my own. In the past, I made decisions without seeking God's guidance, but looking back, I believe that every step, every experience, and every person I encountered along the way was placed there with divine purpose. Only God knows how He directed my journey—from meeting the Master Chief in Memphis and enlisting in the Navy, to being stationed in Winter Harbor, Maine; crossing paths with Ron; facing illness while in service; coming under Chief Cousins' supervision; seeking counsel from the military Priest and receiving care from the military doctor; being honorably discharged; and ultimately moving to California.

None of this was part of my plan, but it all led me on a journey that fulfilled a purpose far greater than anything I could have imagined. This journey and these experiences deeply rooted my faith. Faith has been, and continues to be, the cornerstone of my growth and success.

God's plan is always at work, even when we don't see it. Sometimes in our journey we fall off the path, but God orders our steps, and if we just stay connected, he will put you back on the right path that he has designed for your life. I believe that every step, every experience, and every person who crossed my path during this journey was placed there with divine purpose.

CHAPTER 7

A New Beginning in California

*In the end, it's about what you achieve and how you grow and
stay true to yourself along the way.*

As the plane took off, I looked out the window at Memphis, watching the city shrink until it disappeared behind the clouds. It felt bittersweet. I took a deep breath and whispered, "Dear God, please take care of me and Adrian. Amen."

Adrian tugged my arm, his little voice full of curiosity. "Mama, where are we going?"

I smiled at him. "To a new home in Anaheim, California, where Disneyland is."

His face lit up. "Disneyland? Are we going to Disneyland?" he asked, eyes wide with excitement.

I couldn't help but laugh softly. "Yes, baby, we are." But deep down, I was thinking bigger than Disneyland. I clung to the hope that California would mean a fresh start for us, a place where we could find happiness and a new beginning.

The plane touched down with a soft jolt, and I felt a mix of excitement and apprehension as we taxied to the gate. The stark difference from Memphis was almost overwhelming. Stepping off the plane, the air felt different, warmer, lighter, like a small promise of hope. Adrian was wide-eyed, clutching my hand tightly as we navigated through the airport. His small fingers curled tightly around mine, his eyes darting around in wonder at so many people rushing to and fro. As we approached baggage claim, I spotted him. Ron was waiting with a huge smile on his face, waving amid the crowd of people, a bouquet of bright flowers in one hand. He looked eager yet nervous. As we approached, his eyes immediately locked onto Adrian. He hugged me tightly. I crouched down to introduce them. There was a moment of hesitation, but then Ron knelt too.

"Hey, buddy," he said softly, his voice steady and warm.

I could see the joy in his expression, and for a moment, my anxiety eased.

Adrian tilted his head, studying Ron for a moment, before offering a shy, "Hi." It was the simplest of exchanges, but it spoke volumes.

Ron helped us with our bags, and we walked hand-in-hand to his car, my enthusiastic heart skipping a beat periodically along the way. As we drove to the new apartment he had moved into in Anaheim a few days earlier, Adrian and I both glanced out the window, amazed at the sights.

The city buzzed with energy. Cars zipped through freeways, people hurried along sidewalks, and the sunshine seemed relentless in its brightness. The rolling hills, blanketed in golden grasses, stretched endlessly against the bright California sky. I marveled at the sheer size of the freeways, the unceasing streams of cars weaving through lanes in organized chaos. Adrian pressed his face to the window, giggling at the sight of cars speeding past us. What struck me most was the scale of everything. From the sprawling cities to the towering billboards advertising adventures unknown, everything felt larger than life. California felt vast, overwhelming, yet somehow full of opportunity.

The two-bedroom apartment was nice, simply furnished, comfortable, and roomy enough for all of us. More importantly, it felt like a place where we could start over. In the weeks that followed, I began the slow process of rebuilding our life. I enrolled Adrian in a nearby school, while Ron familiarized me with the city, sharing his routines and favorite spots. He was patient and endlessly supportive, doing everything he could to help us feel at home. Yet, adjusting to this new chapter was not without its hurdles. My body, still fragile from years of strain, reminded me that starting over was not as simple as moving from one place to another.

A few weeks after settling in, I made an appointment at the VA Hospital to address my health issues. The doctors were thorough. After evaluating my symptoms, they still couldn't determine the cause, so they prescribed hormone medication to help ease the persistent bleeding I'd been experiencing. To my relief, the treatment began to show results, and I started feeling stronger with each passing day. However, during follow-up visits, they continued to recommend that I undergo a hysterectomy as a more permanent solution. The suggestion weighed heavily on me, and I grappled with the decision, unsure how to proceed. Each day became a delicate balancing act of caring for Adrian, navigating my health recovery, and confronting the bigger question of what I wanted for my future.

Once we settled into our new apartment, I wasted no time looking for a job. Since Ron was already working in Buena Park and we only had one car, finding a job nearby made sense. One of the places I applied was a Memphis-based company with operations in California that manufactured shortenings and oils. Coincidentally, I had once played second base for their women's community softball team back in Memphis, so I made sure to mention that on my application. But ultimately, it came down to whether I had the skills they were looking for: shorthand and typing.

I felt prepared for the interview. They needed someone who could do eighty words per minute in shorthand and sixty in typing. The tests were a breeze, and by the end of the interview, they offered me the job: executive secretary for VP of Sales and Marketing with an annual salary of $13,500, nearly double the most I had ever earned in Memphis. I was the only Black woman in the executive offices. This job was a fresh start and an opportunity to build a better future for Adrian and me, and I was determined to make it work.

Then, in March, during a routine check-up, the doctor congratulated me. Confused, I smiled and asked, "Congratulations? Why?"

He looked at me knowingly and said, "You're pregnant."

"Really?" I replied.

He confirmed it, and although I wasn't sure how to feel, I smiled and said, "Yes, yes, this is really nice."

When Ron came home from work, I met him at the front door.

"Guess what?" I said. "We're going to have a baby."

His face lit up. He grabbed me, lifted me off the ground, spun me around, and kissed me. "A baby!" he exclaimed.

"Yes," I said, laughing.

His next thought was practical. "We better get married. That way, the insurance will cover everything."

I wasn't sure how to feel at first, but deep down, I was happy. I knew Ron wanted children. I had a great job, and now we were starting a family. Ron was a wonderful person, and I knew we would be happy. Plus, Adrian was about to become a big brother. Ron was from a big family, and he was excited to get married and have a wedding. Me? I liked to keep things small. I told my family back in Memphis, but none of them came. Mama was not thrilled about the whole thing, but she did make me the most beautiful hat for my wedding day. She still held out hope that I would go back to Ernest, even though he had already moved back to his hometown in Prattville, Alabama. Daddy, on the other hand, wished me well and said he couldn't wait to meet Ron in person. Charlett promised to visit later in the year.

We rented a wedding chapel at a church in Anaheim, and I wore a gorgeous purple gown. Ron's brother, Tom, was his best man, and my new neighbor and friend, Linda, stood as my maid of honor. We got married on March 26, 1977, three months after I had moved to California. There were about seventy-five people there, including more than fifty members of Ron's family, along with a few of his friends, my coworkers, and his colleagues from Pepsi-Cola. It was such a happy day. I was about three months pregnant at the time, and our guests could definitely tell.

I was over the moon with my new life: a new job, a new home, and a fresh start on the West Coast. It felt like the start of something special. Ron and I had so much fun together, and I was completely in love with him and the life we were starting in California. He loved me, he was good to me and my son, and that was everything.

I continued working and loved every minute of it. Though my official title at work was secretary, I handled the responsibilities of a salesperson. I thrived in the role, and my boss took notice. He became a mentor, teaching me about the business, which I eagerly absorbed. His belief in me fueled my excitement and passion. Each day, I looked forward to going to work, excited to learn something new, like how to read stock market ticker tapes and purchase commodities like pork bellies. I even filled in for my boss when he was out golfing. He and Norma, the previous secretary who was recently promoted to sales manager, invested time in training me.

Thrilled with how quickly I picked things up, my boss gave me more responsibilities. Although I thought he was grooming me for advancement, I later realized all the attention and added responsibilities created opportunities for him to spend more time golfing. With my growing knowledge of the business, I would call him with updates as the market shifted, and he would guide me on what to purchase.

My coworkers respected me and valued my contributions. Unlike in Memphis, where people tended to segregate themselves, our team in California was diverse and close-knit. Everyone worked together, and there was little division between racial or cultural groups. I truly felt happy at my job. As I settled into my new life and job, my pregnancy seemed to progress quickly. By twenty-six weeks, I looked like I was nine months along. Despite this, I had no trouble working. I loved my stylish maternity clothes and embraced my new life in California.

Adrian was doing well in school. His and Ron's relationship gradually developed into a strong bond resembling that of a father and son. Ron had taught him how to ride his bike, a proud milestone for both of them. However, the process didn't come without its challenges. Adrian was reluctant to fully open up, often hesitant to place his trust in Ron. Ron remained patient and consistent, finding small ways to connect with Adrian, such as helping with homework and taking him to the movies. Meanwhile, Ron and I thrived as a couple. We genuinely enjoyed each other's company, whether it was sharing quiet evenings at home or exploring new places together, and our relationship was loving and fulfilling.

One afternoon, while chatting with the ladies in accounting after lunch, I suddenly felt a rush of fluid running down my legs.

"Her water broke!" one of the women shouted. The office buzzed with concern as they gathered around me. They called an ambulance. As I sat waiting, I knew this was serious; it was far too early for the baby to arrive.

When I got to the hospital, I was rushed to the emergency room, where doctors quickly examined me. They informed me that I was carrying twins, but heartbreakingly, their lungs had not developed enough for them to survive. I could feel them moving inside me, a bittersweet reminder of life floating inside of me. I was overwhelmed with sadness that they were going to die as soon as they came out. Later that day, I delivered both babies. Ron and I were in tears as we gazed through the window in the nursery at our two little babies, one with a light complexion, the other resembling a chocolate chip. They were completely formed, tiny, cute, yet not alive. We held them, cried for them, and grieved the loss of what could have been.

Ron walked me back to my hospital bed, wrapped me in a loving hug, and whispered, "Baby, I am so sorry this happened."

I nodded, fighting back tears.

"Me too," I replied.

Together, we decided to name the little boy Marvelle and the little girl Rachelle. A few days later, we held a small burial ceremony, laying them to rest in Westminster Cemetery in Orange County. It was a moment of deep sorrow, but it was important to honor them. The weeks that followed were difficult. At home, I mourned their loss and tried to come to terms with the pain. Eventually, I came to believe that perhaps this was meant to be, no matter how devastating it felt. Still, I knew how much Ron wanted children. So, I made the silent decision to stop using contraceptives and let my body take its natural course.

Returning to work after five weeks was an adjustment. Mentally, it took some effort to refocus, but my coworkers were incredibly supportive, showering me with encouragement and kindness. Their warmth made me feel truly welcomed, something I had not experienced in Memphis, where workplace segregation and limited interaction between Black and White employees was still common. It became clear to me that moving to California had been the right choice.

A couple of months after returning to work, I learned that one of the salespeople had quit. Excited by the opportunity, I couldn't wait to tell my boss that I wanted to apply for the position. But he didn't come into the office that day. The next morning, filled with anticipation, I went straight to his office, ready to share my plans.

When I told him I intended to apply, he smiled widely, then said something that left me stunned: "I can't recommend you for this position."

At first, I thought he was joking. Laughing nervously, I asked, "You're kidding, right?"

He shook his head.

"Who's going to do what you're doing for me if you leave?" he said.

I reassured him it wouldn't be a problem. I could train someone new to take over my role. "Besides," I added, "I am barely doing secretarial work anymore."

But my boss wasn't persuaded. He sighed, looked down, and said, firmly, "No." Then, he continued, "You don't have a degree, and this position requires one. Plus, you're not ready for the role yet. I can't keep losing assistants. Norma just got promoted, and now you're looking to move up too. It's not the right time for you."

He explained that I needed more experience and that I had only been working a little over a year.

"Maybe next time a position opens up, I'll consider you. But not this time," he said.

My heart sank. His words stung. I couldn't believe I was being held back again. Fighting back tears, I stepped back and said, "Really? After all the hard work and effort I've made in learning this job, this is how you're going to treat me? I can do both jobs, just give me a chance!"

My boss barely glanced up from the papers on his desk.

"If it's a raise you're after, I'll make sure you get one," he said. "But the sales job? Not yet. You're smart, but when you obtain your degree, we can revisit this. I'll speak to HR today about a raise because you deserve it."

Offering me the raise didn't soften the blow. I had worked hard, and he knew I could do that job. I was furious. Who was he to decide my future? Later that day, I marched back into his office.

"Thank you for the raise, but it's not enough," I said, sitting across from him. "Today, you reminded me just how important it is for me to go back to school and get my bachelor's degree. So, thank you, but no thank you. I'm going to use my GI Bill to return to college. No one will ever deny me a job because I don't have a degree."

Ron and I had bought our first home in Pomona, and I was pregnant again. This was a big move, and I had no idea how we were going to make ends meet, but I trusted that my GI Bill benefits would help cover the costs so I could go to college full-time. After we moved, I picked up a part-time job at a department store while enrolled at Mount San Antonio College to complete some general education courses.

When my daughter Maronya was born on June 6, 1978, I stayed home briefly, but financial strain quickly set in. I had to decide: return to work, go back to school, or try both. During that time, I found joy in reading JET Magazine for Black culture and news, and Reader's Digest for practical advice. One August afternoon, an article in Reader's Digest about future careers caught my eye. It highlighted systems analyst as the top job in 1978, a role blending business and computer science. I was hooked. The article listed universities offering programs, including Cal Poly Pomona.

I visited Cal Poly the next day, applied, and prepared to start in January 1979. As a California veteran, the process was straightforward. Though not all my credits transferred, my previous coursework helped me manage the load. Financially, things were tough, so I pushed myself, taking up to thirty-two units per quarter instead of the usual eighteen. I also worked part-time as a programmer, juggling school, work, and family. Sleep was scarce, but I was determined.

On December 31, 1980, I graduated with a bachelor's degree in computer information systems. It wasn't about the degree but about proving I could shape my future. Within a month, I received fifteen job offers. I chose a local job at General Dynamics as an estimating and pricing specialist because the office was within walking distance from home, making life easier for our family.

On my first day at work, I walked into a cramped office filled with five older White men. Their desks were jammed together, offering no privacy. The phone had a lock to prevent unauthorized calls, and files were stacked high on padlocked cabinets. As I stood at the door, one man looked up and asked, "Who are you?"

When I introduced myself, he snapped, "It's 8:01 a.m. We start at eight o'clock. You're late." Stunned, I looked for my desk, but there was none. He pointed to a small desk by the filing cabinets and said, "You can use that until we find a spot for you." I felt like an afterthought. Memories of growing up in Memphis and being made to feel "less than" came rushing back. Was it because I was Black, a woman, or both? Whatever the reason, I wasn't going to let it break me. But I couldn't shake the feeling I had made the wrong choice taking this job.

At lunch, I went home and called ARCO, a company I had turned down for a programmer analyst role paying $19,000, more than the $17,500 I'd be making at General Dynamics. Shirley Reagan, a sharp Black woman who led the department, had been disappointed when I declined. On the phone, I admitted my mistake and asked if the offer was still open. To my relief, she said yes, but I would have to start the next day. I explained I didn't have a car.

"Take the bus," she said without hesitation. That was all I needed to hear. I didn't return to General Dynamics and instead called my boss, resigned, and prepared for my new role at ARCO. The next morning, I dropped my daughter at the babysitter, Ron drove me to the bus stop, and everything fell into place. That day marked the start of my IT career.

In the 1980s, IT was booming. Computers were transforming industries, and personal computers were making tech more accessible. To succeed, you needed skills in programming, systems analysis, and the latest tech. Opportunities were everywhere, but being a woman in IT and breaking into this male-dominated field was a challenge. Gender bias was constant, societal expectations were limiting, and professional networks for women were rare. I had to prove my technical skills and work twice as hard to be seen as capable. Resilience and adaptability were essential. Inspired by women breaking barriers, I refused to let biases define me. Together, we chipped away at stereotypes and paved the way for future generations.

While at ARCO, I joined a program that covered tuition and books, thanks to encouragement from my co-worker and future business partner, Michelle Matti. Michelle was pursuing both an MBA and a law degree and stressed the importance of an MBA for moving into management. Her advice reminded me of the job where I was denied a sales role for not having a degree. Determined, I enrolled in the University of La Verne's MBA program and completed it in two years.

With my MBA, I quickly found new opportunities. After three years at ARCO, I became a Program Manager at First Atlanta Bank of Georgia. It was a chance to step into leadership, but it required moving back to the South. Though hesitant, I took the role after family discussions. Ron stayed in California to sell the house while I moved to Atlanta with the children.

When I arrived in Atlanta, it was clear the city still struggled with racial divides. Although there had been progress for Black professionals, the shadow of Southern racism lingered. At First Atlanta Bank, I developed an IRA Dividend System to retain key accounts with one of their large clients. However, my role was overshadowed by a discriminatory manager whose behavior made the job unbearable. After meetings with HR, I transferred from under his leadership, but his institutional knowledge meant I still had to interact with him.

Fearing sabotage and tired of the bias, I negotiated a move back to California. Though Atlanta was making strides in diversity, the prejudice I faced made it clear the South was not ready for real change. I stayed for eight months, long enough to finish the IRA project, but declined a full-time management role. Once the project wrapped, I returned to California with a clearer vision for my career and life.

Back in California, I joined IBM under a VP in their new Global Services Division. Although IBM's training shaped my management style, I quickly realized I was undervalued. Despite my experience and master's degree, I was hired as a systems analyst II, while less experienced White male colleagues held higher roles. My supervisor, a man with only three years of experience and a Sociology degree, was already up for a promotion two levels above me. Frustrated, I realized I had not negotiated well when hired, eager to move on from Atlanta. I decided to prove myself before addressing the inequity.

Three months into the new role with IBM, I noticed I was gaining weight. Soon, it was confirmed—I was pregnant. After Raymond was born in October of 1984, I took six weeks of maternity leave and then went back to work. I brought in additional revenue, helped IBM grow its professional services, and even contributed to my executive manager earning a spot in the exclusive "100 Club" for top-performing leaders.

It was a busy time, so I decided to address my compensation with my boss. After building up my confidence and accomplishments, I finally sat down with him and asked for a promotion and a $10,000 raise, something I felt was more than fair and reflective of all I had contributed.

My boss heard me out but shut it down.

"Martha, it doesn't work that way at IBM," he told me. "You have to pay your dues through tenure."

I wasn't happy, but I didn't give up. Two weeks later, I approached him again, and his answer was the same. That's when I realized that even at a company as respected as IBM, there were institutional barriers that could hold me back no matter how much I delivered. It was a wake-up call, a moment that taught me the importance of standing up for myself and knowing when to walk away.

Soon afterward, I got an offer to join a Transportation Company as a quality assurance manager. When I told my boss I was leaving IBM, he immediately offered me exactly what I had asked for in the first place, but by then, it was too late.

"The other company I am going to work for recognized my value from my resumé and a few conversations," I told him. "You, on the other hand, had firsthand experience with my work and chose not to act. I am not going to let you or anyone else control my career. This is your loss."

Over the years, I would often run into my boss from IBM at tech events. He was a larger-than-life figure and always commanded attention. Whenever he saw me, he would give me a big hug and tell everyone nearby how letting me leave IBM was "one of the biggest mistakes" he ever made. He would recount the story of losing one of his best employees, and while he seemed genuinely regretful, I stood beside him quietly proud of the decision I had made. That experience taught me to never let anyone dictate my future. I knew my worth, and I was not going to settle for less than I deserved.

Understanding your value is crucial. One of the most impactful lessons I've learned came from a mentor I would meet some years later, Vance Caesar.

"If you ever feel like you're giving more to a company than it is giving back to you, that's a red flag," Vance once told me. "You will never be happy in that situation."

He also warned that the reverse—when a company feels like it's giving more to you than you are giving back—creates tension too. Either way, if that imbalance is not addressed, things can get unpleasant for everyone. If you feel undervalued, that's a sign that it's time to make a change. Do not settle. Remember, you were actively searching for a job when you landed your current one, so why not search again if things are not working? Your ability to secure your current role is proof that you can succeed in finding the right opportunity elsewhere.

During my time at IBM, I met one of my best friends, Camille Richardson. We were both systems analysts and the only two Black women working in the Orange County IBM offices. In fact, there were only four women total, so we naturally bonded. Camille has been a constant source of encouragement and a true champion of my growth throughout my career. Even after I left IBM, she stayed and made sure to keep my old boss updated on what I was up to. Every time I visited the office, Camille's joy was infectious. She would proudly walk me around, introduce me to her coworkers, and say, "This is my best friend who used to work here, and now she's a vice president!" Her unwavering support reminded me of the courage it took to leave IBM, believe in myself, and take that leap into a new chapter of my life. Her pride in my accomplishments has meant so much to me.

While I am deeply grateful for the training and experience IBM provided, I had an unrelenting desire to grow faster than the company's opportunities allowed. I valued everything I had gained at IBM, but it became clear that staying would limit my progress. Sometimes, the bravest move you can make is to step away and pursue the career and life you envision. What is equally important is having a plan B for when things don't unfold as you had hoped. Walking away was a bold decision, but it was also the best one for my growth. I thoroughly enjoyed my time there, but it was time for me to spread my wings and take the next step in my career.

Lessons in G.U.T.S.

Building the career and life I wanted wasn't easy; it took a lot of reflection, big decisions, and plenty of courage, especially after moving to California. It all came down to calling on the principles I have relied on during pivotal moments. My G.U.T.S. helped me tackle challenges, embrace change, and stay true to my values and aspirations. These principles have shaped my journey and reminded me that success is about achievements, growth, and staying authentic along the way.

G — Gratitude: Even when things didn't go my way, I have learned to find gratitude. When my boss passed me over for the sales position, I was crushed. But in hindsight, that moment pushed me to pursue a college degree, which completely changed my life. Similarly, my time at IBM was a rollercoaster. Although I didn't always feel my loyalty was appreciated, I refused to let anyone else dictate my future. I am thankful for the lessons I learned and let them fuel my dreams.

U — Unity: Nothing beats a warm, inclusive work environment. California offered a totally different atmosphere. People embraced differences, and everyone's perspective was valued, which felt refreshing at work, in restaurants, and at social gatherings. Respect and unity lead to stronger teamwork and better outcomes. Unity creates a space where people feel respected and motivated. That kind of energy is contagious and exactly what I knew I would find in California.

T — Trustworthiness: Trust begins with you. Be honest, act with integrity, and believe in your ability to make sound choices. If my boss at IBM had been honest when he hired me, he would have given me the title and salary I deserved then. After knowing the level of my performance, when I asked for what he knew I deserved, he should have done the right thing by me, but he didn't. It was unfortunate for him and IBM that I had to quit before he offered me the promotion and salary I earned with my performance and commitment. It was important for me to honor my acceptance of the new position, even after he matched my new offer. When you keep your word, people learn to trust and respect you. Trust is earned by consistently doing what's right. Know your value and stand firmly on the principles of integrity and honesty, and you'll always be able to feel good about yourself and the decisions that you make.

S — Spirituality: Looking back, I can see God's hand in every twist, turn, and lesson of my journey. I moved through several roles, and with each transition I prayed—and God gave me the courage to step out in faith. My faith has been my anchor. While change often brings fear because of uncertainty, I chose to move forward in faith. And when fear crept into my mind, I met it with prayer and trusted God to lead me.

CHAPTER 8

Elevating My IT Career with a New Attitude

Success is rarely a solo victory. Only when you recognize and honor the contributions of those who travel the path with you can success be truly fulfilling for everyone involved.

When I pulled into the office parking lot on my first day as manager of quality assurance at National Transportation Company, the building didn't exactly blow me away. It was modest and unremarkable, not the kind of place that screams innovation. After spending years working in sleek high-rises at ARCO and IBM, this was quite a change of scenery. But hey, with a $20,000 pay raise, I was ready to dive in and make it work.

When I accepted the role, I didn't really know what quality assurance was, so I knew I had some serious catching up to do. My first stop was the local public library. This was before the days of a quick Google search and endless YouTube tutorials, so I had to dig deep into books and reference guides to figure out what I was walking into. After a few hours of research, a lightbulb came on. QA was not just about fixing problems after they happened, which was my initial assumption; it was about preventing them altogether. This role was about being proactive, not reactive, to ensure quality at every stage of a process, building compliance and trust, staying competitive in the marketplace, and ultimately improving profitability. Once I understood the bigger picture, my confidence grew.

Even though QA was unfamiliar territory for me, it didn't feel completely foreign. At its core, it had similarities to the IT projects I had worked on, so the goal was the same: to deliver something that meets customer needs, stays on budget, gets done on time, and ticks all the right boxes. That familiar framework gave me a foundation to build on, and I started to piece things together. Of course, there were moments of doubt, times when I felt overwhelmed, and days when I second-guessed my ability to succeed in a role I had no formal background in. But I relied on my skills, my willingness to adapt, and my belief that I could figure things out if I worked hard enough.

I have always believed that with good research, an open mind, and a little self-confidence, you can tackle anything. The powerful combination of knowledge and belief in yourself can push you past what you think you are capable of and help you achieve more than you thought possible. Not knowing everything on day one turned out to be a blessing in disguise. It forced me to step outside my comfort zone, to learn, adapt, and grow in ways I hadn't anticipated. That experience shaped the way I approach challenges to this day. I didn't have all the answers when I started, but I trusted myself to figure it out. That trust, paired with my determination to learn and improve, was all I needed. Sometimes, diving headfirst into the unknown is the best way to discover what you are capable of.

As quality assurance manager, I served as the link between operations and the tech team. To design systems that improved efficiency, I first had to fully understand operational needs. Once I had a clear picture, it was up to me to make sure the IT team built applications that met those needs, securing approvals and overseeing thorough testing at every stage, not just at the end. My role was critical to the success of IT projects. If I didn't fully understand the job, how could the IT team?

So, I took full ownership of my responsibilities and introduced new processes for software development.

Introducing approvals and testing at different stages of development was new and not exactly welcomed. Most programmers and IT staff weren't thrilled to add more policies and procedures, and the quality assurance manager wasn't always the most popular person in the room. Still, I was determined to make a positive impact and set us up for success. My experience with large-scale applications had taught me how to manage tight deadlines and complex requirements. I knew changes like these were not always easy or immediately accepted, but necessary. Ultimately, it was about ensuring we delivered the best results possible.

Success is always possible, but it doesn't happen magically; it takes a plan, confidence, and G.U.T.S. I had the ability to do the job, but I needed a framework to learn it properly and ensure exceptional performance. After researching, I found a quality assurance certification program that seemed like the perfect fit.

Early one Monday morning, coffee in hand, I headed to the CEO's office. My boss, Matt, had told me he had an open-door policy for any concerns or ideas I wanted to bring to his attention. When I arrived, he was on the phone but motioned me to come in.

As I stepped into the massive space, I took in the grandeur of it. Dark, polished mahogany furniture filled the room, exuding an air of wealth and distinction. Floor-to-ceiling windows overlooked the city, and delicate decor pieces accented the room, adding an air of grace and order. The setting was impressive, almost intimidating. I thought, *One day, I'll sit in an office like this.* Matt, a short man who seemed even smaller amidst the towering furniture, ended his call and joined me at a large conference table that could easily seat twenty. Despite the imposing environment, he greeted me warmly, as usual. His friendliness always put me at ease.

I handed him a printout of the conference materials and explained, "Since this is a new focus area for the IT industry, gaining the proper credentials and certifications in QA will greatly benefit both me and the company."

He glanced at the papers briefly.

"No problem. Sign up for the course, call HR to arrange your travel, and go."

I was stunned by how quickly and decisively he approved of my request. As he stood up, he looked at me with genuine curiosity and asked, "Are you happy with your decision to join us here?"

I stood as well and replied confidently, "Yes, I am. This is going to be a great place to work, especially knowing I have the support of my boss." He smiled, and I left his office feeling both encouraged and motivated.

Walking back to my modest, standard-issue company office, I thought, *You need to make this work, Martha. You owe it to yourself to succeed.*

The training was exactly what I needed. It provided both theory and practical tools like templates, policies, and detailed guidance on defining roles and responsibilities within the new IT department. Beyond the technical aspects, it gave me a clear framework to approach my role methodically, making challenges easier to tackle and expectations clearer. After completing the program and earning my quality assurance management certification, my confidence skyrocketed.

Back at the office, I was ready for whatever came next. Despite resistance from the IT team and others, I stuck to the new plan and made sure it was implemented. My high standards and expectations caught the team off guard since they were not used to working under that kind of pressure. Some of them went to Matt and said they couldn't keep working with me because they thought my expectations were too high. Nevertheless, the systems and processes had been established, and the transformation succeeded. It was a challenging experience that underscored the importance of persistence, leadership, and the ability to drive change in the face of resistance.

The CIO called me in for a major discussion afterward. I stood my ground, explaining that I had been tasked with delivering a project with an aggressive timeline, and it was completed exceptionally well.

"Yes, the work was excellent," he said, "but you burned out the team. Now, they're calling you a dictator with no compassion, and you no longer have a functional team."

I responded plainly, "You can't impose ambitious demands with tight deadlines and expect everyone to like you while still getting the job done."

The reality was that the IT employees hadn't been pushed to perform at high standards with deadlines. Until this project, the IT environment had long accepted mediocrity.

"It was tough to bring in new processes and effectively build some standards, but I did move the bar with a successful delivery of a new system, on budget and on time," I continued. "Those employees who leave will carry a valuable experience to their new job, and those who stay will deliver new projects at a higher performance level because they experienced success. You now have a stronger team and with a thorough knowledge of Quality Assurance."

With that, I got up from my seat and stormed out of his office, frustration burning within me. Receiving that criticism wasn't easy, but it ended up being a turning point in my career.

A few weeks after that conversation, I reflected and realized there was room for me to grow as a leader. I came to understand that success could be achieved with a greater sense of compassion. I realized that if I wanted to succeed, I needed to focus on results and also on building a strong, collaborative team. I thought about the feedback and recognized how my previous approach might have impacted the IT team.

Determined to take action, I called a meeting with the entire team to address our challenges openly. That morning, more than thirty-five employees gathered in the large conference room, and I began with a simple yet honest statement: "I'm here to make a difference, and to do that, I need to hear from you."

As I looked around the room, I could sense the tension; it was tight and uneasy. I noticed a few employees who I knew had been the most vocal about their frustrations. Rising from my seat, I walked through the room and spoke directly to them and the rest of the team.

"To be fair," I said, "I'm not sure I'll achieve everything I hope for today, because many of you don't trust me or even believe I care about what you have to say, but I do. I really do."

I returned to my seat, pulled out my notepad, and began reading aloud a few comments and concerns anonymously submitted by team members prior to the meeting. To my surprise, some of the statements were genuinely funny, and as I read, laughter rippled through the room. I joined in, and slowly, the atmosphere shifted. People began to relax, chatting quietly among themselves.

When I finished reading, I spoke again.

"I care deeply, and I want to make a difference. So, give me a chance. Let's start fresh. I can't change the past, but I want you all to know that there is a new chief leading this company now. We're under real timelines and deadlines, but I believe we can meet these challenges together."

I paused, letting my words sink in, then continued.

"Today, I'm taking off the hat of the dictator you may see me as, and I'm stepping into the role of your leader. I'll be implementing policies and procedures designed to help us succeed, especially as we bring on new program managers and consultants. Together, we can avoid stumbling over ourselves and reach our goals. But it starts here, with us working as a team."

By the end of the meeting, the tension had eased, and for the first time in a while, I felt renewed energy in the room. It was a small but meaningful step forward. To further my efforts to make things right, I began meeting one-on-one with each team member to hear their thoughts and to show them that I was committed to learning and improving. When the company was acquired, the investors were all about return on investment, a big shift for many employees. I had to get on board with these new goals while still keeping my team's trust and morale intact. I had to find a way to balance corporate demands while supporting my team, all under tight deadlines.

This was my first real challenge as a manager, and it taught me that managing a team is different than managing my own schedule as an employee. I had to make some changes, even if I didn't yet know what they would look like. But one thing was obvious: my success depended on my team, and to support them, I had to level up my communication and leadership skills.

That realization, and that project, became the starting point for my growth as a leader. I took their suggestions to heart and applied them to future projects, maintaining strict deadlines and accountability while also fostering a more supportive and collaborative environment. Some employees chose to leave, but most stayed. Together we became a high-performing, dynamic team. This experience transformed my leadership style and taught me the importance of balancing results with empathy.

The Power of "We" vs. "I"

Success can be a dangerous pursuit when it becomes centered around "I" instead of "We." On my journey toward achieving my goals, I overlooked the human factor, the people who were as integral to the process as I was. While there are moments in life when it must be about you, not every situation warrants that mindset. In my new job, it *should* have been about "we". This role required teamwork, and there was no way I could achieve success without the team's collective efforts. Success in this context needed to be shared by everyone and not owned by one person.

Initially, my approach was all about me, myself, and I. My only focus was making this new job successful. I was determined, and I believed I would achieve my goals at any cost . . . and to some extent, I did. The project was a success, but not because of me alone. It succeeded because of the incredible team that worked alongside me. Yet, while I celebrated, they felt defeated, overlooked, and unappreciated. That was not success for the whole.

From this experience, I learned that success is not a solo journey. No one achieves greatness alone. As English poet and scholar John Donne wrote, "No man is an island." Every success requires the help, effort, and collaboration of others. Beyond reaching the finish line, true success is about considering the people who help you get there and making sure they feel valued along the way.

Lessons in G.U.T.S.

Stepping into management within an emerging discipline was a significant transition. I felt prepared to face the anticipated challenges with a sense of purpose, confidence, and G.U.T.S. However, the role fundamentally shifted my focus from personal accomplishments to guiding a team toward collective success. This proved more demanding than I had imagined. It taught me the necessity of humility and pushed me to develop a more inclusive leadership style to effectively drive results.

G — Gratitude: Gratitude has always been my foundation. I'm deeply thankful for the lessons I learned early in high school—like how to research by heading to the library to gain knowledge to improve my shorthand. That same approach guided me as I learned Quality Assurance. It was at the library that I discovered the Quality Assurance Institute in Orlando, FL, and the courses that helped me embrace this new discipline. My boss invested in my development, funding my preparation and trusting in my potential. I am so grateful that his mentorship was genuine as he offered me invaluable wisdom that strengthened my leadership and people skills.

U — Unity: Success is never achieved alone. After we completed the project, it became clear that unity was essential to our success. I learned that leadership can make or break a team, and the way you treat people directly influences their loyalty and commitment to future work. Inviting and acting on feedback leads to more harmonious outcomes. While a directive, authoritarian style can deliver short-term results, it often breeds fear, intimidation, and anxiety. Leading with humility and genuinely valuing people's opinions—even when you don't adopt every idea—creates stronger results because the team feels respected and engaged. Ultimately, leadership style is a defining factor in management: when people are treated with respect, teams become more unified and success is shared by everyone. Unity is about knowing when to reach out, collaborate, and build an inclusive foundation of support from everyone on your team.

T — Trustworthiness: After my boss shared how the team felt post-project, I was deeply disappointed in myself. While I was celebrating the win, my team was struggling with my leadership style. Regaining their trust became my priority. When you make mistakes, you have to look inward, be honest, and commit to change. For me, the first step was bringing everyone together to express my sincere desire to earn back their trust and respect. I gave them space to share how they truly felt, and I laid out how I would work more collaboratively provided we could all be honest and open to doing things differently. Trust goes both ways: their honesty earned my respect, and my honesty and humility earned their trust. Over the next year, we worked together in a new way and we were highly successful.

S — Spirituality: Forgiveness matters when you've hurt others or they believe you've wronged them. Focusing only on yourself can lead you to ignore your mistakes and avoid apologizing. A true apology means setting aside your pride and asking for forgiveness. It only takes one person to apologize, and that's all God requires. If those you've offended don't accept your apology, that's okay. Forgiveness doesn't require reconciliation; reconciliation takes at least two people. When reconciliation does happen, it fosters lasting peace for everyone. I was fortunate that my team accepted my apology. After meeting with my team, I felt at peace and God blessed me with even greater success.

CHAPTER 9

Rising to New Heights

Success is never built on cheating, dishonesty, or harm to others. There is enough opportunity in this world for everyone. True success comes from walking the right path, no matter how challenging it may be.

After nearly two years at the National Transportation Company in San Gabriel Valley, we had successfully completed the major projects on our plate. Around that time, my boss took on a new role with the same group of investors, relocating to Minneapolis. About six months later, he reached out with an intriguing opportunity to join his new company, Cable Valued Network (now known as QVC Shopping). There was a catch, though: I would need to work as a consultant and commute to Minneapolis every week. To sweeten the deal, he offered to cover my travel expenses and pay me $65 an hour, a compelling offer compared to the $80,000 annual salary at my previous job.

The timing was perfect. A friend from ARCO and I had already been discussing the idea of starting a consulting company that specialized in finance and IT. The friend, Michelle Mattie, had recently become a new mom and decided to stay home for a while to prepare for the California bar exam. Our new venture allowed me to work as a consultant under our company's banner, Mattie and Scharf Management Consulting.

Four weeks later, I walked into the new CIO's office to deliver some bittersweet news.

"I've truly enjoyed my time here," I began, "and I was looking forward to continuing. However, I've been offered an opportunity to further my quality assurance career at a much larger company, and I've decided to take it."

Steven, the CIO, looked at me with clear disappointment.

"I've already heard that you'll be joining Matt in Minneapolis," he said. "I was actually planning to promote you to Director of Planning. Would you consider staying on in that role?"

His offer took me by surprise, but in my heart, I knew the position wouldn't align with the career growth I envisioned for myself at Cable Valued Network.

"I truly appreciate the offer, but I believe this new role is the best step for me right now."

He nodded and wished me well as we shook hands.

I left his office feeling a mix of sadness and excitement. The transition would not be easy. Traveling weekly and being away from home would be a challenge, but I decided to take the leap before committing to a permanent position that might require relocation. I wanted to test the waters and give myself six months to decide if this path was sustainable. My children were my top priority. Adrian had started eleventh grade, Maronya was eight, and Raymond was two years old. I wasn't ready to uproot them until I was certain it was the right move.

That evening, after dinner, I sat down with Ron to break the news.

"Ron, I quit my job today," I said, bracing myself.

He looked at me, startled. "You did what?"

"I quit," I repeated, "because I'm taking the consulting job in Minneapolis that my boss from the National Transportation Company, Matt, offered me."

Ron and I had talked about this possibility before. It wasn't exactly ideal, but we both agreed it could work for a while. The pay was great, and we figured we could manage the temporary setup. It was a big decision, but I felt ready to take on the challenge and see where it might lead. Now, moving to Minneapolis? That was a topic we had never touched. Knowing how much Ron loved his job at Pepsi, I knew that conversation wouldn't go over well. So, I decided to hold off on bringing it up until it was necessary. Instead, I shared the part I was excited about.

"I negotiated a schedule where I'll work Monday through Thursday and can take a flight out on Thursday evening and return on Sunday nights," I told him. Thankfully, we had Judy, our amazing live-in nanny, so I figured this plan could work, at least for a while.

Ron got up, heading toward the family room to watch TV, and simply said, "We'll make it work. Go for it." His calm support was reassuring.

I went upstairs, filled with excitement, to say goodnight to my children. As I visited each of their rooms, it hit me: I wouldn't have these precious bedtime moments with them while I was in Minneapolis. Kissing and hugging them goodnight had always been a special part of my day, and now I would be missing that. I lingered longer than usual, taking deep breaths as tears welled up in my eyes.

The next morning, I called Matt in Minneapolis and said, "I'm ready to start."

His immediate response was, "When will you get here?"

I booked my flight for Sunday and began preparing for this exciting new chapter. There was a lot happening at a TV Shopping Company on the technical front, and when I arrived, a significant hiring push was underway. Matt, now the senior CIO, had earned a stellar reputation among the executives and investors. However, things were not as smooth behind the scenes. The IT managers had a different perspective.

As I spent more time with the team, it became apparent that tensions ran high, and my role as director of quality assurance would be challenging. There was an obvious disconnect between the CIO and Matt, the senior CIO, who created an unfavorable resentment from the team he had hired. It was clear they didn't like him at all.

Despite the challenges, I worked hard to build strong relationships with the entire team. Still, as time went on, the friction between the CIO and Matt only grew, making my work at the TV Shopping Company increasingly complicated. Yet, through it all, I remained committed to fostering collaboration and finding ways to navigate the tension. The experience was both demanding and rewarding, a true test of my resilience and adaptability.

One morning, about five months in, I was in Matt's office when an employee rushed in to inform us that a major earthquake had struck Southern California, centered in Northridge. My heart sank.

"Oh my God, my children!" I screamed.

Frantically, we turned on the news, trying to understand the extent of what had happened. Panicked, I ran back to my office and called the airline to book a flight to California. I repeatedly dialed home, but the phone lines were jammed. With each failed attempt, my anxiety grew. Tears began streaming down my face as I said aloud, "I can't reach them, I can't reach them! Oh my God, please!"

Matt came by with an update, assuring me that most of the damage was concentrated in Whittier, CA. Still, I kept calling until, finally, my nanny, Judy picked up the phone. She was crying and screaming, "I'm scared, Señora Martha!" My heart raced as I asked about the children.

"Maronya has been crying for you nonstop, calling your name," Judy said. I told her to contact Ron and ask him to come home immediately, assuring her that I would be on the next flight back.

When I arrived home that night, I was relieved to find minimal damage to our house. However, Maronya was deeply shaken. She had already been struggling with my absence since I started commuting to Minneapolis, but the earthquake had traumatized her further. I stayed home for the next two weeks, and during that time, I made a critical decision: my family needed to move to Minneapolis with me. It was the only way forward.

I called Matt and expressed my desire to take the position as an employee. The company agreed and offered me a relocation package.

The wheels were set in motion for the move. Ron, however, was resistant. He didn't want to uproot our lives, but he also understood that this opportunity was transformative for our family. The financial benefits of the position were significant, so, reluctantly, he agreed to the move.

The sacrifice was immense, but I stood firm in my decision. I accepted the position, and in January 1988, the entire family, including Judy, moved to Minneapolis. The transition wasn't easy. Adrian was set to graduate from high school in June, and moving mid-year was a difficult adjustment for him. Still, I felt in my heart that relocating to Minneapolis was the right choice for everyone. I knew it was necessary for the well-being of my family and for our future.

Once again, I found myself faced with a difficult decision. After much consideration, I arranged for Adrian to stay with friends in California until he graduated from high school, but he chose to join us in Minneapolis instead. It worked out for a while. Ron began applying for jobs in Minneapolis, but his heart wasn't in it.

We sold our home and purchased a spacious, beautiful house in Maple Grove, the largest we had ever owned. But despite its grandeur, it was not a cheerful home. Ron struggled to adjust to the move and went months without work, which led him to feel depressed. He had over thirteen years of dedicated professional experience with Pepsi Cola but lacked confidence when it came to interviewing somewhere new. Fear kept him from pursuing job opportunities, which only deepened his depression. Unfortunately, he refused to seek professional help to overcome his struggle.

While Ron's struggles weighed heavily on us, I thrived in my new role as director of database administration and quality assurance. I collaborated closely with Matt to implement critical policy changes. Meanwhile, Matt applied pressure on our team. Internal resistance made progress challenging and slow. Some colleagues actively sabotaged initiatives that would have benefited them, simply because they were reluctant to embrace change. The friction was undeniable, forcing me to tread carefully in order to remain effective.

One weekend, a catastrophic system failure brought the company's operations to a standstill, resulting in significant financial losses. Senior executives were livid, and the blame landed squarely on the IT team and Matt. I was tasked with investigating the root cause of the failure and my findings exposed negligence on the part of Peter, the CIO, and Larry, director of data center operations.

When I presented my findings, Peter and Larry urged me to conceal the truth, suggesting I label it a system error. That put me in a difficult position. I had carefully navigated the political dynamics between Matt and the broader IT team, but this was about integrity. Despite the pressure, I refused to misrepresent the truth and shared my findings honestly. As a result, I went from being a trusted colleague to an outcast. I was excluded from meetings and even the casual happy hours we'd once enjoyed.

The fallout didn't stop there. Tensions between Matt and the executive team escalated. Soon thereafter, Matt was fired. One of the company's investors arranged for him to return to California, where he took on a new role at another company. While the experience was challenging, it underscored the importance of standing by my principles, even in the face of adversity.

When the TV Shopping Company announced its sale to QVC, I decided to stay with the company during the transition. One morning, Peter called me into his office.

"Martha, we have reorganized and eliminated your position," he said. "Therefore, I've assigned you to handle special projects."

He then looked at me with a smirk and added, "You won't need a staff or an assistant. I've reassigned them, and you also won't need an office in this area."

I was furious. Standing up, I asked, "Is that all?"

He smiled and replied, "I think that's enough for now."

Shaking with anger and humiliation, I left his office and went straight to the director of HR to express my frustration. As I poured out my emotions, even shedding tears, the director listened kindly, then said, "I stopped him from firing you outright. I understand your frustration, but he does have the authority to reorganize his operations. You can stay until you decide it's time to leave."

"Really? There's nothing you can do?" I asked. He merely shook his head. I walked out of the office feeling disheartened.

At that moment, I resolved to make sure the executives understood the importance of hiring someone truly qualified for the senior CIO position. I scheduled a meeting with the chief administrative officer (CAO), Bobby, and explained how my demotion was a direct result of doing my job efficiently. While I wasn't sure if he believed me initially, the situation soon proved my point. Over the following weeks, the company's systems experienced repeated failures. Bobby called me to his office to ask for my insight.

"You need proper supervision," I told him plainly. "Hire a senior CIO to manage this team until the company transitions through the acquisition."

He agreed and assured me he would contact an agency immediately. Within two weeks, a new senior vice president of IT was hired who immediately focused on improving the efficiency of the data center operations. I reported directly to him. As a team, we developed and implemented new processes and procedures that were immediately put in place. While resistance to change created tension, the new senior vice president of IT evaluated the current IT operations and realized that there were some critical negligent operations, and Peter, the CIO, was fired. In the end, it felt like a strategic chess game, and I had achieved checkmate.

Lessons in G.U.T.S.

This experience taught me the importance of integrity. Friendships or personal grievances should never compromise trustworthiness or professionalism. I also learned to navigate workplace politics at a high level, always with integrity and without malice. My goal was never to harm anyone, but rather to safeguard the company's success. Despite my demotion, I persevered and delivered lasting improvements, avoided taking sides, and carefully worked with all teams to implement necessary changes.

Every time I approached the CIO's office, I could sense his frustration. Yet, I remained professional, knowing I held the upper hand. Gradually, I earned the respect of employees and other directors who recognized the unfairness of my initial treatment. I turned the situation around for myself, my family, and the company. By the end of this journey, I no longer felt humiliated. I felt victorious. I gained the respect of the TV Shopping Company's executive management and achieved greater success by doing the right thing. Upon my departure, the new senior vice president shared with me how much he had appreciated my integrity, which ultimately became the cornerstone of my professional triumph. Success comes to those who have G.U.T.S.

G – Gratitude: Gratitude has always been a guiding principle for me, especially when navigating injustice. I am thankful for the self-restraint I have learned to practice, which allowed me to act with integrity even when facing retaliation for exposing leadership negligence. Though it was a difficult path, I am grateful that executive management ultimately recognized my actions were in the company's best interest. This outcome was possible thanks to the foundational mentorship of my history teacher, Nat D. Williams, who taught me that true change comes from within, not from anger. The principles and training I received early in life provided the strength to maintain my professional convictions and see this process through to a just resolution.

U – Unity: Unity is a powerful force; it can be used for good or misused for harm. I saw our IT leadership team, aware of its own inefficiencies, band together to resist change and obscure the truth when technical problems arose. They pressured me to join their efforts to conceal the issues. I tried to collaborate and implement improvements, but when I began reporting problems accurately, I was no longer seen as a team player. True unity means aligning with people who act with integrity and purpose. I learned that, regardless of the consequences, you should stand with those doing what's right. Never compromise your principles just to belong.

T – Trustworthiness: Trust really is the foundation of strong character. If you want to have G.U.T.S., you've got to lead with integrity and honesty—be trustworthy and trust others, too. Those two things are non-negotiable for lasting success. I learned that the hard way. I refused to cover up for IT leadership. In meetings, I told the truth about the problems, and because of that, I became an outcast and was demoted by the CIO, Peter. But despite the consequences, I still believe honesty is always the right path. The executive team respected me more for it, even while I was dealing with the humiliation under Peter. And ultimately, Peter was dismissed because of his dishonesty. When I left the company, I walked out with respect and my head held high. Any success achieved without honesty and integrity isn't success at all; it's failure, no matter how profitable it might look.

S – Spirituality: I believe dishonesty cultivates habits that only lead to further wrongdoing. I found myself working with an IT leadership whose morals did not align with my own. Despite my attempts to encourage change, my spiritual commitments to God prevented me from compromising my character with dishonesty. Saying no was essential. As we advance in our careers and goals, temptations to overlook our moral principles will always exist—whether for money, status, or a dishonest opportunity to excel. Yielding to these temptations ultimately prevents an enjoyable success and displeases God. In contrast, telling the truth brings peace, a clear conscience, and pleases God. Therefore, I chose the path of integrity.

The Beginning of Entrepreneurship

You are never alone on your journey. Lean on your networks,
trust your instincts, and keep moving forward.

On a chilly November morning, when the blistering Minneapolis cold had started to hit hard, my former boss Matt called me out of the blue. He'd just become a senior VP at Columbia Savings and Loan in California and wanted me to join him. He knew the TV Shopping Company had been sold and it wouldn't be long before I'd be out of a job in Minneapolis. He had reached out to me a few times before, right after he left the company and things got tough for me.

"Are you ready to come back to California?" he asked.

My stomach dropped, my heart raced, and before I could think, I said, "Yes, absolutely."

The timing couldn't have been more perfect. Ron and I were already talking about moving back. We had a new house, mounting expenses, and Ron was earning far less than he had in California. He was struggling in Minneapolis, and the strain was starting to show in our marriage. I hated the idea of staying in Minneapolis, but I was torn because we had just purchased the new house.

Matt offered a temporary role as Director of Database and Quality Assurance while he worked on opening a CIO position for me. The only catch: he needed me to start in a week. That meant leaving the kids in Minneapolis until Christmas.

That weighed on me, but I knew I had to do it. When I got home and told Ron we were moving back to California, I expected him to be excited. Instead, he looked worried and disappointed.

"What am I going to do?" he asked.

"You'll find a job there, maybe even go back to Pepsi," I said. But he was not as thrilled as I was.

Maronya, eleven at the time, was over the moon excited to return to California and our nanny Judy actually cried tears of joy; we'd helped her get her citizenship in Minneapolis, and she had more friends and opportunities waiting for her in California.

The hardest part was breaking the news to Maronya that I had to leave for a few weeks before she could join me. She cried so much. I held her, hugged her tight, and promised her I'd be back before Christmas, which made her smile.

It wasn't an easy decision, but I knew what I had to do. As much as I didn't want to leave my children again, I knew I had to make that sacrifice to get closer to my goals and to help my family thrive. Moving back to California was the opportunity that would help me achieve both objectives. The next day, I resigned from my job and bought a ticket to Orange County.

When I arrived at Columbia Savings and Loan, the office I was nice but operations were in disarray. The CIO didn't yet know I was there to replace him and thought I'd be reporting to him. I started interviewing his team to figure out how to fix the neglected operations and get things running smoothly again. Within weeks, I was managing a team of forty-five and untangling the company's inefficiencies.

By Christmas, I had arranged a rental home in Orange County and flew back to Minneapolis to bring my family home. Maronya had her little suitcase packed and was ready to go. Finally, we were home again. I swore I would never leave California once I returned.

Meanwhile, my marriage to Ron was barely holding on. Ron was struggling to adjust and decided to start his own business, a restaurant delivery service called "The Delivery Zone." It was visionary, essentially what UberEats, DoorDash, and GrubHub are today, but the business drained what little savings we had left. He was frustrated and adrift, and our marriage began to buckle under the strain.

By January 1990, I was officially promoted to CIO and First Vice President. I had gone from earning $19,000 as a programmer in 1981 to $130,000 in a little over eight years. Columbia Savings & Loan was constantly in the news since it was the main bank supporting junk bonds. One of my key tasks was to separate the bank's operations and all banking activities from those of the Beverly Hills investment group. It was a tough challenge, but we pulled it off.

Professionally, I was thriving. On the flip side, my personal life was falling apart. With Ron's failing business and repeated refusal to seek counseling for himself and our marital challenges, I was exhausted. I couldn't keep putting all my energy into him and his dreams. Raymond was six, and Maronya was thirteen. I didn't want to hurt them, but the emotional toll this was taking on all of us was too much. After fourteen years of marriage, Ron and I divorced. I did my best to support the children emotionally during the divorce. They knew their father loved them, and I explained that we would still be a family, just in a different way.

Then, things changed dramatically at work. The bank's heavy involvement in junk bonds and high-risk takeovers caught up with it. When the junk bond market collapsed, Columbia followed. As a result, Resolution Trust Corporation (RTC) and the Federal Deposit Insurance Corporation (FDIC), both government entities created to manage failed banks and savings institutions, took over the institution.

Right before the takeover, the senior executives started resigning. The corporate offices were in Beverly Hills, but I worked at the data center operations in Irvine. Matt called me into his office one day.

"The Feds are going to take over in a few days, and I'm resigning today. But you can stay on until you find another job," he said.

I was confused.

"What do you mean?" I asked.

He explained that the government would run the bank until it was sold. He assured me that I would be okay.

"They don't really understand this business," he said, "so you'll be here for at least a year before they figure things out." As he spoke, he frantically packed up his office to leave.

Sure enough, two days later, the Feds showed up, and everything changed.

The remaining VP-level staff entered the conference room, where there were about eight people to greet us. One older gentleman stood up, put on his glasses, and began reading a scripted statement announcing that the government was now in charge and that we all reported to them. Then he asked, "Who's in charge of the computers and data?"

I spoke up, "I am."

He looked at me and said, "Stay after the meeting."

After everyone left, he asked straight-up, "Are you planning on staying on the job?"

"I plan to, unless you feel otherwise," I said.

He smiled and said, "If there's anyone we need right now, it's you." Immediately, I started to relax. He explained how important the data was to the takeover's success.

I smiled and said, "Sir, I've got a great team, and we'll support you through this process. How long do you think it'll take?"

He replied, "About six months to a year."

I negotiated to keep my team, and he agreed, with one condition: If anyone quit, I couldn't replace them. I accepted and immediately called a meeting with my staff, assuring them we'd have about six months of work and advising them to start looking for new opportunities. I stayed on as CIO, and my team became the FDIC's go-to experts for managing the junk-bond data from failed savings and loans across California.

My leadership didn't go unnoticed. An FDIC executive suggested I start my own business to support the ongoing operations and warned me that if I didn't, the work would likely be handed off to a large accounting firm. That conversation planted the seed of entrepreneurship in my mind. It was 1991, and although I didn't have the money to start a business, I knew this was an incredible opportunity.

I'd never seen myself as an entrepreneur, but I thought, *Why not?* I reached out to Thomas Ballantyne, a savvy businessman and co-owner of two IT staffing companies, DPRC and BCSI, and laid out the opportunity over lunch. He immediately saw the potential and proposed a 51/49 partnership, emphasizing the value of starting a minority woman-owned business to tap into growing opportunities for minority-owned companies.

We'd use one of his inactive companies, Information Management Resources, Inc. (IMRI), to get started quickly. We shook hands, and in 1992, IMRI was born.

I didn't have capital, but I had experience, determination, and faith. A few weeks later, Tom's attorney sent the contract. With guidance from my friend and mentor Betty LaMarr, I negotiated a clause giving me 85 percent of my bill rate on any consulting work I personally performed. I sent the revised contract back to Tom's attorney, signed it, and officially became the majority owner of Information Management Resources, Inc. on April 1, 1992. Yep, April Fool's Day!

At forty, recently divorced, undergoing counseling, and recovering from personal bankruptcy, I poured everything into building IMRI. Our first consulting contract came from the FDIC itself, followed by small projects with Bank of America and ARCO. Tom preferred staffing deals—quick, low-risk placements—but I loved consulting. Consulting let me solve problems, lead projects, and create value beyond billable hours.

During a meeting one day, I told Tom, "Staffing is your expertise, not mine. I'm a consultant, and that's the business I want to focus on."

"Why the hell would you want to do that?" he said.

His tone was sharp and caught me off guard.

"Because I'm good at it, and I know I can make good money," I said.

He argued that consulting was risky and that staffing was simpler. Just send someone to do the job, no deliverables required.

I nodded and said, "I hear you, Tom, but that doesn't challenge me."

It was obvious we didn't see eye to eye on the business model, but by then, I had learned not to push too hard. Instead, I focused on making things happen and dealing with the fallout later. I took on the role of salesperson recruiting and placed several people as contractors at ARCO and other companies. Still, my heart was set on finding business opportunities where I could offer consulting services.

When Tom and I started, we agreed I would take a modest salary. He set it at $40,000, which wasn't ideal considering I had been making $150,000 at Columbia Savings & Loan. But I was so excited about the opportunity that I didn't push back. I figured I would manage for a few months until we brought in enough business to support a better salary. Still, I wondered how much sacrifice I would need to make and how long I could make that arrangement work.

As the FDIC lawsuit ramped up, the workload grew, and I realized I needed staff and a proper computer setup to handle all the reports the law firm was requesting. We needed a reliable data center and some former employees from Columbia Savings & Loan to help us. I brought in Kathy and Tom Weeks, who had worked for me at the bank, and Percy Hall, a telecommunications expert who also worked for me.

We rented a tiny office in Santa Ana and fired up our equipment, only to blow a transformer and knock out power to the whole block. Percy sat in my office, calm as ever, saying, "It's okay. I'll fix it." We hoped no one else in the building would connect the power outage to our operations. Percy became one of my greatest assets, and Kathy and Tom were just as loyal. They understood the systems and knew how to handle the accounting, which kept us moving forward.

Eventually, the FDIC asked us to relocate operations to their Costa Mesa facility and consolidate with their data center, and about six months after that move, the FDIC ended our contract. By then, though, IMRI was up and running with about six employees.

During that time, we secured a major contract with Bank of America after they merged with Security Pacific Bank. The executive who had once encouraged me to start my business had since moved there, and about a year later, he called with an extraordinary opportunity. That deal was a game-changer for us.

After the 1992 merger with Security Pacific Bank, Bank of America needed to close numerous branches across California, Arizona, Nevada, Washington, and Oregon, one of the largest consolidation efforts in banking history. Because of our proven track record, IMRI was awarded the project for California, Arizona, and Nevada. It was a turning point; revenues soared, and our team grew quickly.

Percy led the consolidation work, and my longtime assistant, Janet Miller, rejoined me to keep operations running smoothly. I was doing a lot of marketing at the time, working with companies like ARCO, Sanwa Bank, and others. Meanwhile, Tom kept pushing me to focus more on staffing. We did land some positions at ARCO and a few other places, but I was struggling financially after taking such a big salary cut. I kept telling Tom, "I need to make more money. This is getting hard for me."

He would smile and say, "After the investment." It was frustrating.

By now, IMRI was gaining traction and making money, but Tom wasn't satisfied. He only cared about staffing opportunities, whereas I loved consulting and delivering IT solutions. That difference in priorities caused a lot of tension between us. He even joked about getting heartburn because of it. Around this time, Mary Ellen Weaver, president of DPRC, the other woman-owned company Tom had a

50/50 partnership with, decided to buy him out. They parted ways, and their agreement included a non-compete clause that stopped Tom from doing mainframe business.

Tom called a team meeting to announce that he was no longer the owner of DPRC and made sure we all knew he came out on top.

"I've made a lot of money from this sale," he bragged. Then, he told the team that IMRI, not DPRC, would now handle all mainframe contracts. He also threw in a sarcastic warning, saying we should "tread lightly" when dealing with former DPRC clients. His explanation felt vague, so I decided to set up a meeting with his former partner to get some clarity.

I was friends with Mary Ellen and admired her; she was smart, confident, and an incredible businesswoman. We met at her office in Irvine, and during our conversation, she warned me not to let Tom use me as a way to get around taking mainframe work from her company. She confirmed that Tom was restricted from doing mainframe work due to the non-compete agreement.

"Martha, don't let Tom cause you legal issues because of his non-compete clause with us. He's not allowed to do mainframe business for the next five years," she said. That finally cleared things up for me.

I shared my target client list and my consulting strategy with her, and she assured me that none of the companies I was pursuing were part of that clause. As we walked toward the door, she gave me a big, beautiful, confident smile and said, "I am getting ready to go for the big payday."

A big payday? I thought. The phrase stuck with me, and as I walked to my car, I played those words over and over in my head. I thought, *I am going to build IMRI fast so I can have a big payday too.*

When I got back to the office, I told Tom about my conversation with Mary Ellen. I brought up the non-compete clause to get his take on it, and he invited me to lunch. We headed over to Caliente, an amazing Mexican restaurant nearby. As we sat down, Tom started talking about how much money we could make together from the mainframe staffing business. He mentioned that my minority status would be a huge driver for the business.

"Stop focusing on consulting work and follow my lead," he said. "You can make more money with less risk if you stick to staffing." Although there was some truth to his point, I enjoyed consulting work. Sure, it was riskier, but I was convinced I could make more money doing it.

"Oh, and one other thing," I said, looking deeply into his eyes. "Mary Ellen mentioned something about a big payday. What's that about?"

Tom immediately dropped his fork and gave me a cold, angry look. In a quiet but sharp voice, he said, "She's going to lose her ass." Then he added, "Don't get any ideas from her. She doesn't know what the hell she's doing." After picking his fork back up, he muttered under his breath, "Yeah, right, a big payday. We will see." I could tell I had hit a nerve, so I didn't bring it up again. But, as I thought back to her smile and the way she said it, I believed her more than I believed him.

At the time, BCSI handled all IMRI's back-office processing. Tom had cosigned my line of credit, and his team at the Irvine office managed all the billing and time reporting. Deep down, I knew that if my minority ownership held any weight, I needed to at least be the one signing the checks. But in reality, I was not in control of anything other than my dream, and even that felt a little shaky in that moment.

Despite the nonstop work, I allowed myself small breaks, taking affordable weekend cruises with close friends.

On one of those cruises, I met Daniel, assistant bar manager on the ship. He told me he went by the name Daniel because no one could ever pronounce his first name, Mathurin, correctly. He was ridiculously good-looking, but dating wasn't on my radar at the time. I was juggling a divorce, a new business, and financial challenges. One night, almost a year later, Daniel and I exchanged numbers when he mentioned he would be getting off the ship to visit a friend in Irvine. A few days later, he called my office and asked me out. I didn't really feel like going out with him. Dating someone who worked on a cruise ship seemed complicated. I called my friend Karen, who took some of those weekend cruise trips with me.

"If you don't want to go out with him, I will!" she said.

That made me laugh, and I thought, *why not?* He was gorgeous, had a beautiful Caribbean accent, and the most stunning smile I had ever seen. So, I picked him up in Irvine, and we went to dinner at a restaurant in the city of El Toro. From our first date in May 1992, I was hooked. This man completely mesmerized me: his looks, how he treated me, his conversation, his smile, everything.

When he asked if I would visit him on the ship when he returned, I hesitated.

"I don't know if I'm ready to start a new relationship," I said.

He looked me in the eyes, smiled, and said, "I didn't ask you for a relationship. I asked if you would visit me on the ship. If a relationship happens, we'll deal with that then. But right now, all I need to know is whether you will visit me."

I couldn't help but respect his honesty and confidence. He had a way with words that completely pulled me in. So, I smiled back and said, "Yes." And the rest? Well, that's history.

After Daniel returned to his work onboard ship, he sent me flowers every Friday. He never got to see them himself, but the florist nailed it every time. Before long, a relationship started to blossom and love quickly followed. We saw each other every other week, and everything fell into place.

Eight months later, on February 20, 1993, we got married. A few of my friends thought I had completely lost it, but I didn't care. I followed my heart, and I am so glad I didn't listen to the naysayers. There were plenty of doubters, including my mom, who thought Daniel might be another Caribbean guy looking to marry an American woman for citizenship. But Daniel proved them all wrong. Thirty-three years of love and dedication, and it is not over yet. Our love will last forever. Daniel was my blessing from God and has become the love of my life.

On the business front, the company had made a small profit, so Tom suggested I get an office in his building. I continued marketing, and a consulting opportunity came up with the Metropolitan Water District (MWD). A few months later, IMRI was awarded the first-ever $1 million contract earned by a minority firm at MWD.

I was bursting with excitement and ran upstairs, rushing into Tom's office.

"Tom, Tom, we just won a $1 million contract to install an Oracle system at MWD!"

I stood in front of his desk while he leaned back in his big chair.

"How many people?" he asked.

Still buzzing, I replied, "It's going to be three to five people for about six to eight months, including me as the engagement manager." I added that, as the engagement manager, I would manage the profit since it was a firm fixed-price contract.

That's when Tom jumped out of his chair, yelling.

"Are you crazy? You're going to lose your ass on this contract!"

It was obvious he didn't think I could handle a consulting project. To be fair, his experience was only in staffing contracts, hiring people by the hour and making a profit on the markup. This was a different ball game.

I looked at him, feeling disappointed.

"No, I won't," I said. Then I walked out of his office, angry that he couldn't celebrate this big win with me.

The contract started, and I began billing for my hours, but when payroll came through, I only got my regular paycheck, nothing for the project work. Confused, I asked the office manager why. After all, my contract with Tom clearly stated I would receive eighty-five percent of my bill rate for any consulting work I did. She looked down and said, "You need to talk to Tom."

I went straight to Tom's office and told him I wanted to get paid for the forty hours I would bill on the project. We went back and forth, but he refused to honor the agreement we had in place. In the end, I agreed that once the company got paid for the billing, I would take my salary out for the hours I worked. At that moment, I was thankful Betty Lamar had encouraged me to include that clause in our company formation agreement. She had warned me that Tom would never do any work but would try to control everything. I needed to find a way out of the arrangement, even though I had no idea how to do it yet.

For the MWD project, Tom suggested I hire a couple he had worked with for years. Once they started, they completely ignored me. The husband began running meetings without me and even met with the client to make decisions on the project without consulting me. When I confronted him, his response was always the same: "I'll send you a report with my invoice."

Thankfully, my friend Leveda Woolery worked for a woman who owned the company that held the Program Management contract for this engagement. Leveda knew this couple and also knew Tom well, and she could see they were undermining my authority. She was not about to let it slide. Meanwhile, I was fearful, worried this whole mess might lead to MWD canceling my contract.

Then one day, Leveda stormed into my office and shut the door.

"Get up!" she said. "You are firing these two people today."

She sat at my desk and started drafting the termination letter herself, then looked me straight in the eye.

"This is over. You are getting them off this project. They are undermining you and trying to convince management that they have all the knowledge," she said.

I had hired a friend from IBM as a project manager, and another incredibly talented project manager was already on board. Leveda was clear: "They can do this work. Call both of them into the conference room and get rid of this problem today."

Leveda and Camille, the project manager, didn't leave it at that. They came into my office like a whirlwind of energy and determination, hyping me up like the strong, fierce women they are. It was like a tornado of confidence, and all I could do was get up and join the fight to take back control. Leveda finished the letter and handed it to me.

"This is your contract, your company, and you are in charge. So, act like it."

I was nervous because Tom had predicted I would fail, but Leveda reignited my confidence. I called them into the conference room and, with authority I didn't even know I had, fired them. Then I met with MWD's project managers and told them they had been let go and would no longer work on this project. I reassured them that I had the right team in my new consultants, and we had all the skills to finish this project. And I did. The project was successful, and I continued working numerous other projects. Over a period of six years, I generated more than $8 million in consulting engagements, and I am still working with them today, more than thirty-two years later. Leveda's push was exactly what I needed to take back control and own my success.

After that incident, Tom and I weren't on speaking terms anymore. I had let go of this couple and redirected all of IMRI project invoices to my office. I hired my own office manager to handle my back-office processing, taking that responsibility away from Tom's office manager. I even started processing my own checks for my consultants. Naturally, Tom's CPA got wind of all this and gave him a call. At the time, the company was doing well and making a profit, but I didn't have my own line of credit at the bank and everything was guaranteed by Tom.

IMRI had moved out of Tom's office on the twelfth floor to a smaller space on the third floor in the same building. One afternoon, Tom stormed into my office, furious. He started yelling, "You cannot do that! You cannot do that! I am going to shut down the line!"

I stood up, and angrily shouted, "Do what?"

He yelled back, "Pay yourself that kind of money!"

I reminded him my contract allowed me to pay myself for consulting work, the same way we paid other consultants.

"I'll pay myself for every hour I bill on a contract," I said. "Go read your contract! Now, get out of my office!"

He left in a huff, but I knew that wasn't the end of our confrontation.

Later that evening, I got a call from Mary Ellen, president of DPRC. She asked if I had my corporate formation contract at home. When I found the contract, she directed me to the clause that gave me the first right of refusal to purchase Tom's shares at the price he offered anyone else.

Then, she dropped a bombshell: Tom had offered to sell her his forty-nine percent stake in IMRI for $1 if she agreed to take over the $250,000 line of credit, which I was in for about $180,000. Mary Ellen then urged me to buy the shares from Tom myself. I asked if she'd consider buying them and going into business with me, but she declined.

"This is your chance to own one hundred percent of your company," she said. "You don't need a partner."

I told her I didn't have the line of credit.

"Figure it out," she said, "even if you have to factor your receivables. I have confidence in you."

An hour later, Tom called. The moment I heard his tone, I knew this wasn't going to be a pleasant conversation.

"I am done," he said. "I asked Mary Ellen to buy me out, and she said yes."

I knew that wasn't true because I had just talked to Mary Ellen. He went on to say his CPA and lawyer would call me the next day to work out the details. Then, he ended the call with a curt, "Good luck."

The next morning, Tom's CPA called me to discuss the deal with Mary Ellen. I told him I was exercising my right of first refusal to buy Tom's shares for $1. He seemed surprised and asked how I knew the offer. I told him that was the price Tom had given.

Ten minutes after that call, Tom phoned me in an angry huff.

"You don't have enough money, and I'll shut down the line of credit today," he said.

Later, his attorney called and gave me sixty days to figure it out. And that was the start of what would become a pivotal moment for me and IMRI.

Mary Ellen told me to figure it out, so I teamed up with Tom's new VP of sales to work out a deal for prepayment on some contracts. Even with that, two days before Tom's shares were finalized, I was still $25,000 short and had no options. I had to pay out the credit line and also give Tom forty-nine percent of the profits that had been earned.

I prayed about it that night, and the next morning I came up with the idea of asking for my invoice at MWD to be paid early. The next morning, I went to MWD's accounts payable manager. Her desk was piled high with papers, and she looked completely swamped.

"Can I sit down?" I asked. She gave me a reluctant glance and motioned for me to sit.

"I am really struggling," I began, explaining that I needed $25,000 to buy out my partner. "Is there any way you could pay my $50,000 invoice early?"

"When's it due?" she asked, barely looking up.

"In two weeks," I replied.

Her tone sharpened. "I can't do that."

I felt a lump in my throat as I pleaded, tears streaming down my face. "Please, I'm begging you. You're my only hope. If I can buy him out, I'll own my company outright." I poured my heart out, explaining everything.

Her demeanor shifted. She stood, came around her desk, and hugged me. "It'll be okay," she said. "I'll do it. I want to see you succeed." She shared with me how proud she was of me as a Black woman breaking into MWD. She said I was the first she had ever seen.

"Get up," she said. "I'll take care of it."

She turned to her monitor and started to work again. Without looking at me she said, "Come back tomorrow at noon."

When I returned the next day, she handed me the check with a smile. "I am so proud of you. Go make it happen."

I hugged her tightly, thanked her, and ran to the bank. The teller credited the funds immediately since it was from MWD, which was a huge relief because the attorney had said the money would be withdrawn that day to pay off the line of credit.

Later, I had a meeting with Gina Price, a program manager at MWD and a close friend. After the meeting, I pulled her aside and explained the situation. I asked if the legal documents could be faxed to her office after hours. Gina, who I commuted with daily on the Metrolink, didn't hesitate to help. That moment was a turning point. The kindness and faith of these women made it all possible, and I'll never forget how they helped me take control of my future.

At around 5:20 p.m., I got a call from the attorney with the news I'd been waiting for. He told me the money had cleared the bank account, and the deal was officially closed. Tom was no longer an owner of IMRI. I rushed to the elevator and headed down to Gina's office on the tenth floor. She and I stood by the fax machine, awaiting the ownership documents, barely able to contain our excitement. Suddenly, the machine started whirring, and the papers began coming through. We both ran over, grabbed the first page, and saw it was from the attorney's office.

I shouted, "Gina, it's happening!"

We stood there, glued to the machine, watching as each sheet of thermal fax paper came through. When it was done, I picked up the stack and verified the deal. Every single share had been transferred to me. Tears filled my eyes. Gina hugged me, and I felt an overwhelming sense of relief. It was over. My partnership with Tom was officially behind me. On that day, Wednesday, June 21, 1994, I became the sole shareholder, one hundred percent owner of Information Management Resources, Inc. (IMRI).

As Gina and I left the building and made our way toward Pershing Square to catch the train back to Orange County, we couldn't stop laughing and talking. All I could think about was how this was one of the happiest days of my life. I was finally the 100% owner of my company. It was mine. No partners. No compromises. On the train ride home, Gina and I brainstormed. She mentioned moving back to Washington, D.C. and suggested we should consider setting up an office there and becoming an 8(a) company to tap into federal contracts.

My mind buzzed with ideas. I couldn't stop daydreaming about the future and the possibilities. I could see IMRI becoming a $100 million company in a few years. We barely made it to the train on time, running to our track at Union Station and hopping on the last train to Irvine. As I sat by the window, staring out at the city lights, my emotions were all over the place: happy, scared, anxious, but mostly excited. I was now my own boss, and the future of IMRI was entirely in my hands.

Not long after, we completed our project at MWD and were awarded more contracts, earning over $8 million in projects over several years. I brought back some incredible people I worked with before, like Camille and Percy Hall, and together, we kept building the business. Gina followed through on her plan and set up our Washington, D.C. office, right in her dining room!

I hired Gina as our first business development person in D.C., and she introduced me to the Small Business Administration (SBA), leading to our acceptance into the 8(a) program for economically and socially disadvantaged businesses. That nine-year program opened doors, landing us contracts with the Defense Information Systems Agency at data centers across seven locations. We started growing our federal business from there.

IMRI was officially on the map. Gina and I made a great team. I would fly out, stay at her home, and we'd work side by side in her home office. She was a blessing, proof that treating people right always comes back full circle. Eventually, Gina needed to move on to a higher-paying job, and IMRI transitioned to a small office in Fairfax County, Virginia. But those early days with her were some of the most rewarding. We embraced every challenge together as we helped IMRI grow.

During that time, I initially knew very little about government contracting and the numerous rules, requirements, and regulations that came with it. Fortunately, when our first 8(a) contract was signed in Columbus, Ohio, I had the privilege of working with a contract officer who oversaw the entire process. Everyone there lovingly called her Tiny, and she was such a huge help during that key moment.

When I first visited Tiny's office, she looked at me and asked, "What type of vehicles do you have?"

"We have an Isuzu Trooper and a Ford Probe," I confidently replied.

Tiny stared at me for a moment and said, "Oh my God, what do I have here?"

I could tell my answer was not what she was expecting, so I tried to fix it by saying, "I didn't know I needed a vehicle for the contract, but if you tell me what I need, I can buy it tomorrow!"

Tiny shook her head and smiled. Then, she asked, "Do you have any other federal contracts?"

"No, ma'am."

She glanced at me over the rim of her glasses and said, "That's what I thought."

It turns out Tiny wasn't asking about my personal cars, she was asking if I had any *contracting* vehicles, ways for the government to buy services from my business. At that moment, she knew I didn't have the slightest clue about government contracting. I was as green as grass. But Tiny didn't make me feel bad about it. Instead, she said, "I guess I'll train you," and that's exactly what she did. Tiny became my mentor, guiding me step by step through my first Department of Defense contract. She pointed me to guidelines, taught me the ropes, and set me on the right path.

Mentorship is one of those things you don't always ask for, but when it's offered, you have to be thankful. Tiny was my blessing; she gave me her time and knowledge, and I'll never forget that. I'll always be grateful for her patience and kindness. She didn't judge me or make it hard for me to learn. I realized I needed to educate myself, so I signed up for classes, read manuals, and studied everything I could about government contracting. I even trained my office manager, Janet Miller, so we could tackle this together.

Janet, my assistant at Columbia Savings & Loan when I was the CIO, was a lifesaver. She was so efficient, and I was blessed that she came back to work for me and was the backbone of IMRI. She did everything, from writing proposals and handling finances to managing time reports and answering phones. Janet even created templates and databases to keep us organized. I don't know how IMRI would have survived without her. Janet was by my side for more than twenty years before eventually moving to Washington State. She was loyal, hardworking, and an absolute rock.

As our federal work grew, so did our commercial projects. I set up a business office in Memphis and hired my best friend, Gerrelynn, who I had worked with at Memphis Health Center. She even got the *Commercial Appeal Newspaper* to write an article about me, which opened up new opportunities. Finally, something positive happened for me in Memphis. Through her, I met Joseph Lee, the City of Memphis CFO, and landed a project to help the city select a new financial system.

For this project, I brought in Martine Sloan, someone I had met in 1985. She was the first female CIO I had ever worked with, and she was a powerhouse. Martine led the Memphis project and many others. She was a fantastic leader, got things done, and didn't mind traveling for work. Martine worked for IMRI for many years, and I could not have asked for a better teammate.

Since 1992, IMRI has grown steadily, and here we are, more than thirty-three years later, having delivered more than $400+ million in IT consulting engagements across the country and internationally. It's been an incredible journey, and it all started on that unforgettable day in June when everything changed and I became one hundred percent owner.

The intimidation from Tom and the McDonalds made me question my leadership, lose confidence, and develop a serious fear of failure. And let's be honest, fear can completely throw you off course. Whether it's in your personal life or at work, the fear of failing is something so many of us struggle with, especially when people doubt us.

Tom planted that fear in me. From the start, he predicted I would fail. He even brought in two consultants he wanted to take over my work because he didn't think I could manage such a big contract. With Tom's support, those consultants tried to take over the project, undermine my leadership, and do whatever they wanted. I felt powerless, and that fear grew until I felt completely defeated. What I learned from that experience is that the only way to beat fear is to take action. Fear of failure is normal, especially when you are being challenged by others. In retrospect, there were three reasons my fear of failure grew so much:

I let other people's opinions mess with my confidence.

I avoided dealing with my fears, which only made them bigger and stronger.

I let fear call the shots and control the direction I was heading.

Recognizing those patterns was a game changer for me. Fear will pop up, but how you handle it matters. It starts with taking decisive action. Sometimes, you have to make bold moves. Letting go of the consultants was risky, but it was the right call for the project's success. It reminded everyone—clients and team members alike—of my leadership and authority. Restructuring the leadership on the project helped me get the team back on track, and that paved the way for growth and success. Every challenge is an opportunity to grow. Reflecting on those experiences can show you your strengths and the areas where you can still improve.

Lessons in G.U.T.S.

Becoming an entrepreneur and finding success was not easy. It took a lot of G.U.T.S. (and yes, a few failures along the way). I had to face my fears head-on, and I quickly realized I couldn't do it alone. Leaning on my network for support made all the difference.

G — Gratitude: I'm deeply grateful for the incredible support system that has carried me through every chapter of my journey. Remarkable people—Gina, Leveda, Camille, Betty, Mary Ellen, Tiny, Martine, Janet, Brenda, Maronya, Vance, Chris, Gerri, Joseph, and the accounts payable manager at MWD—showed up for me in different seasons, offering love, friendship, professional guidance, and encouragement exactly when I needed it. My greatest blessing has been my husband, Daniel, who has stood by me from the very beginning and remains by my side through both the highs and the lows. I wouldn't have made it without them.

U — Unity: My friends, mentors, and the people I really looked up to turned out to be some of my greatest assets. I was surrounded by good people, and treating them with kindness came back to me in ways I never could've predicted. When I needed them the most, my friends really stepped up. They encouraged me, shared their wisdom, and had my back when I felt vulnerable. It's made me see how important it is to have good people around you, especially when life throws its curveballs. Having that support made all the difference. Success is never achieved solo; there is always someone there who helped you even if it's in a small way.

T — Trustworthiness: Doing the right thing is essential to earning respect and trust. My business partner was far more financially secure than I was and knew I couldn't support my family on the salary I was receiving. I was working full-time in the business while he wasn't actively involved. As I increased our revenues, the right thing would have been to adjust my salary to align with what I had previously earned. Instead, he refused, creating confusion and forcing me to enforce our partnership agreement, which significantly adjusted my income. This escalated tensions and ultimately made the partnership hostile. Had he acted fairly from the start, we could have avoided the split. Once trust is broken, collaboration becomes difficult. Undermining me by encouraging others to disrespect my authority further eroded trust. In any partnership or relationship, maintaining trust requires mutual respect, honest communication, and consistently doing what's right for everyone involved.

S — Spirituality: God always has a plan, even when we cannot see it. The Bible teaches that what is impossible for man is possible with God. He sent so many people to help me gain ownership of IMRI. Mary Ellen was the cornerstone—her selfless spirit gave me the opportunity to purchase my business. Leveda encouraged me when I felt defeated at MWD. Betty offered the wisdom to include contract clauses that allowed me to retain a portion of my billing rate so I could pay myself. Janet supported me with unwavering loyalty. Gina opened her home to serve as our Washington, D.C. office. God was orchestrating my success long before it became visible. I believe that while we make our plans, it is God who orders our steps and governs the outcomes. When you treat people with love, that love often returns—sometimes from unexpected places. Trusting the Lord as your guide helps you navigate difficult paths through prayer and thanksgiving. When you believe in God, you are never truly alone—He is always with you.

CHAPTER 11

Being the Only One

*Being the only one in any situation can feel daunting, but it
is also an opportunity to grow, learn, and make an impact.
Never underestimate the power of your unique voice and
experiences; they hold the potential to inspire change and make
a lasting difference.*

I registered IMRI as a Minority Woman Business Enterprise (MWBE) in both Los Angeles and the State of California to qualify for set-aside contracts, part of a special program designed to promote diversity and inclusiveness. These contracts are exclusively available to small businesses that hold specific certifications, like being Disadvantaged-Owned, Woman-Owned, Minority-Owned, or Service-Disabled Veteran-Owned.

Orange County, however, did not participate in set-asides at the time. Whenever I went to LA for events, my Black colleagues would ask me, "How on earth do you think you can run a successful business behind the 'Orange Curtain?'" They had a point: Blacks made up less than one percent of the population back then and only two percent today. However, I was not intimidated.

I had worked for IBM in Orange County, so I knew the lay of the land. The only problem was that I didn't have any business there yet.

So, I set a goal to start marketing IMRI in Orange County. At the time, IMRI was only the second Black IT company and the first Black woman-owned company in Orange County. To get connected, I joined the local chapter of the National Association of Women Business Owners (NAWBO) and quickly realized that I needed to get involved in the community.

Shortly after I started IMRI, I got a call from Irene Kinoshita, the owner of Ascolta Training in Irvine. Irene is an Asian woman and a fellow minority in the community. From the moment we met, we connected. Deep down, I think she knew I would need some help navigating the community, so she reached out right away, and I am so grateful she did. She wanted to connect as a fellow technology business owner and minority woman entrepreneur, so we grabbed lunch. She was so warm and welcoming, and we quickly became great friends.

Irene didn't stop there. She introduced me to a network of women in Orange County, which was such a huge support for me in those early days. She also introduced me to golfing. Now, Irene was way more serious about the sport than I was, and today she's an amazing golfer whose handicap is probably a nine! She encouraged me to take lessons so I could get better, and with her support, I did.

Over the years, Irene and I have supported each other in both business and life, fostering a friendship built on mutual respect and shared ambitions. Many times, at events, Irene and I were the only minorities in the room. Together, we have worked to create a meaningful impact in our community, mentoring young girls, empowering fellow businesswomen, and giving back through both time and resources.

One time I attended an event hosted by the Orange County Business Journal to honor the Women Who Mean Business award recipients. The keynote speaker was Dr. Judy Rosener, known for being outspoken about women's rights and diversity. She was a professor at the University of California Irvine School of Business and the author of *Ways Women Lead*. From the moment she stepped on stage, I could tell she was different. She wore a hot pink suit with matching lipstick, her gray hair standing out against her bold, colorful look. She was about five foot, seven inches tall and full of energy.

As she gave her speech, Judy didn't hold back. She called out the business community for being so slow to promote women and minorities. Then, in the middle of her talk, she suddenly looked directly at me and said, "It's a shame that there is only one Black person in this audience of over 500 people." I could feel every head in the room turn to look at me. But she wasn't done. She turned around, glanced at the stage behind her, put her hand on her hip, and said, "And it's a damn shame that we are at a women's event, and everyone on the stage handing out the awards to these women is a man."

The audience was stunned. You could feel the tension in the room, but then the women started applauding . . . loudly. Judy was bold, blunt, and unapologetic. As she wrapped up her speech, she turned to Richard Reisman, the publisher of the *Orange County Business Journal*, and said, "I am sure I won't get invited back to speak again, but next year, Richard, you better fix this problem and get some women on this stage." I was blown away. She was a powerhouse, and I instantly liked her.

When her speech ended, the women in the room gave her a standing ovation. Afterward, I introduced myself to her, and as soon as I did, she said, "Call my office. I want to get to know you." I walked away from the group of women gathered around her, already making a mental note to follow up. That moment stuck with me, and I thought, *One day, I'm going after the Women Who Mean Business award.*

A few weeks later, I met with Dr. Judy in her office, and she completely blew me away again. She was lively, outspoken, and fiercely liberal. We talked about everything: politics, Black issues, women's issues, you name it. The more we talked, the more I admired her. After that, she'd call me a couple of times a month to chat. She even nominated me to join the International Women's Forum (IWF), LA Chapter, Trusteeship, which is an exclusive, invitation-only group connecting women professionals from all fields. I have been a member now for more than twenty years, and through it, I have gained recognition and visibility and built amazing friendships and relationships.

It took a few years, but eventually, I did win the prestigious Woman Who Means Business award. I had been nominated several times before, but in 2000, I was finally selected as one of the five winners. My speech was short and emotional. I shared a bit about my dream and what the award meant to me. I noticed tears in the eyes of many women in the audience, mostly White women, as there were only a few Black women in the room. But their tears felt genuine.

As I walked back to my seat, I pictured Nat D. Williams's face, smiling and shaking his head, saying, "I told you so." I had broken barriers, not by being radical, but by working within the system and creating change from the inside. At that moment, I felt accomplished and proud as a business owner and for thriving in an environment that could have been hostile but turned out to be supportive. It was truly an honor.

Being the "only one" in certain spaces wasn't always easy, but it taught me about resilience, connection, and breaking barriers. I have learned that resilience is not about avoiding tough situations or pretending negative emotions don't exist, it's about figuring out how to handle them and keep moving forward.

One of the biggest lessons I have picked up is the power of building relationships, especially with people who are different from you. For me, that meant stepping out of my comfort zone and connecting with people who did not look like me or share my background. Whether it was being the only woman, the only Black person, or the only tech professional in the room, I realized that instead of feeling intimidated, I could use those moments to stand out. People are naturally curious when you are the "only one," and that curiosity often opens the door for conversations and connections.

From a young age, I was never one to shy away from speaking my mind or standing out. I always found myself at the forefront, never lingering in the background, and I rarely let anyone intimidate me. Even as a child, when White people acted as though they were superior, I wasn't afraid to call it out. There were plenty of moments when my mom worried about the consequences of my confidence. That unwavering confidence and innate belief in equality stayed with me and allowed me to stand strong and feel equal to others in any room I walked into. So, I started seeing those situations as opportunities. I embraced the chance to meet new people, share my story, and learn from theirs. And you know what? Some of those connections turned into meaningful, lasting relationships. Being the "only one" is not a disadvantage, it's a chance to explore, network, and make an impact.

After I received the award and gained some publicity, Dr. Judy introduced me to Michelle Jordan, a Crisis Communications Marketing Expert. Michelle was incredible, a true connector and a passionate advocate for women around the world. She recommended me for a mentorship opportunity with C200, an organization dedicated to supporting and advancing women entrepreneurs. Through that program, I had the chance to work with two phenomenal mentors. Lurita Doan, a former GSA Administrator appointed by President George W. Bush, taught me the importance of celebrating my successes—especially the small ones—because they pave the way for the bigger achievements. I also had the privilege of learning from Pamela Coker, the CEO of Acucorp, Inc., who left a lasting impression on me.

As my business continued to grow, I met another extraordinary woman: Barbara Taylor. We initially connected while I was recruiting for a project manager position with the City of Costa Mesa. Although that role didn't work out, Barbara and I formed a lifelong friendship. She and I joined together as co-authors of my first book, *Year 2000: On the Other Side of Midnight*, and she even worked as a consultant for IMRI on several projects. IMRI emerged as a trusted partner in navigating this crisis, leveraging its expertise in information technology and systems management to help organizations identify, address, and mitigate Y2K-related risks.

Barbara introduced me to her friend Jan Norman, an editor at the *Orange County Register*. Jan came to my office and interviewed me for an article about me and my company. I was carpooling to work with Daniel a few weeks later and asked him to stop by the grocery store so I could grab a copy of the paper. I put a quarter in the newspaper stand, pulled out the paper, and was shocked to see that I was on the front page! The headline read, "How to Exceed Your Wildest Dreams," and had a huge photo of me. I looked at it and thought, *Wow, I actually look pretty good!* I couldn't believe my eyes.

"Daniel, look at this!" I screamed.

I flipped through the paper and found another full-page section about me. I kept saying, "Oh my God, oh my God," as Daniel drove us to work. My entire body trembled as I read the article. The title was a bit misleading, but the story explained it beautifully. When I got to my office, I sat there, looked up, and said again, "Oh my God."

That article changed everything for me in Orange County. So many doors opened because of that one article and all the incredible women who supported me along the way. The article was syndicated in multiple cities, including Oakland, Pittsburgh, and Columbus. Then, out of the blue, I got a call from Gloria Zigner, the society editor for *Orange Coast Magazine*. She started the call with, "Hello Martha, who are you? I don't know you." Her tone threw me off, but I knew right away she was someone I needed to know. She introduced herself, invited me to speak on her radio morning talk show, and told me where and when to meet her.

I went to meet her at the recording studio, and there she was, a beautiful redheaded Jewish woman, full of life, colorful in her conversation, and nice. She talked to me about the article and let me introduce myself during the taping. Gloria insisted that we go out to lunch soon thereafter; we did, and that lunch turned into a friendship. She became one of my mentors and strongest advocates in Orange County. If Gloria Zigner was not in your Rolodex back then, you were not really part of the who's who in Orange County.

Through Gloria, I met Ruth Ko, the Editor and Publisher of *Orange Coast Magazine*. Ko (as she insisted I call her) was a gorgeous, petite, smart Asian woman with a network that seemed endless. She knew everyone in Orange County. Every issue of her magazine had a celebrity on the cover, and Gloria's society column was where everyone wanted to see their name and face. Gloria and Ko were best friends, and they adopted me into their circle, making it their mission to introduce me to Orange County, rolling me out in the magazine, and making sure I attended all the important events, parties, and gatherings. Thanks to Gloria and Ko, Orange County got to know Martha Daniel.

Soon, I was invited to join the Women's Round Table of Orange County (WROC), a group of high-profile women who networked and celebrated each other's successes. I was the only Black woman in the group, and often, Daniel and I were the only Black couple at the majority of events in Orange County. Whenever Daniel and I walked into a social event, we always felt like we belonged there, because we did indeed belong.

I was so glad that my high school teacher, Nat D. Williams reinforced this mindset. He taught us Black history and instilled so much pride in his students' accomplishments. He made it clear: Never hang your head, never bow down, and never let anyone make you feel less than. He showed his students that we were just as smart and capable as anyone else. Those lessons stayed with me and have shaped how I carry myself to this day. When I walked into a room of mostly White faces, I always knew my worth. That's just who I am.

For years, I was often the only Black person in the room, whether at events, meetings, or social gatherings. It wasn't always easy, but I learned how to make the best of the situation, especially since networking was key to growing IMRI's business. If you ever find yourself as "the only one" in the room, here are some tips to help you feel more at ease:

1. **Be confident**: You belong there. Walk in with confidence, be approachable, and work the room. People will notice you; it's

hard not to when you are the only one, and many will feel more uncomfortable than you do. Take the lead. Shake hands, introduce yourself, and let the conversations flow. Most people will be curious about who you are and how you ended up there, and that's your chance to shine. Use this to your advantage and network your way toward your goals, whether it's landing new business, advancing your career, or simply making valuable connections.

2. **Be assertive**: I like to scan the room first to figure out which group I want to approach. If you know who's hosting the event, start there. If not, look for the person leading the conversation in a group; they are usually the key connection. Walk up, extend your hand, and introduce yourself. It might interrupt the conversation for a moment, which is fine, but it draws attention to you and creates an opening to join in. Once you are in, relax and contribute to the discussion. I usually avoid approaching only one person, it's easier to join a group of two or more where the conversation is already flowing. Remember, people are as curious to meet you as you are to meet them.

3. **Be comfortable**: Don't let being the only one weigh you down. Relax and be yourself. Focus on asking questions rather than offering all the answers. It's more important to learn about the people you are meeting and decide who to follow up with later.

4. **Know when to move on**: Don't linger in one group too long unless it's really worthwhile. When it's time to leave, say, "It was great meeting you," and, if you have found someone you want to stay in touch with, let them know by saying, "I'll keep in touch." No need to overthink it; just move on to the next group and repeat the process.

Lessons in G.U.T.S.

Being in a room where you are the only one who looks like you can be tough. It is also a huge learning opportunity. It's challenging, yet it's a chance to build resilience, make meaningful connections, and sharpen the skills that lead to success. The biggest takeaway is to stay focused and confident in yourself. When you do, networking gets easier, and you'll naturally create a presence that feels approachable and non-intimidating.

G — Gratitude: I'm deeply grateful that my mother and father taught me to love myself. My parents always made me feel special, which gave me strong self-esteem. Because of that foundation, I rarely felt intimidated even when I came face to face with discrimination. I'm also thankful for my mentorship with Nat D. Williams, which helped me defuse hatred and learn how to adapt to different environments rather than feel afraid or inferior to anyone. Thanks to my upbringing and mentorship, I became comfortable in any setting, met incredible people, and built lifelong friendships. I'm especially grateful for the friendships I've formed with people from all walks of life and race— many of them I met when I was the only Black person attending the event. Friendship should never be limited by race or ethnicity. The people who helped me succeed came from diverse backgrounds. True friendship has no race, color, or ethnicity; it's universal. The people who've helped me succeed came from all different backgrounds, and I am grateful I learned early to love and accept everyone. True friendship has no race, color, or ethnicity; it's universal.

U — Unity: Unity isn't about always fitting in, it's about finding connection, even when you stand out. Being the only one in the room doesn't mean you're alone; it means you're surrounded by people who might look or think differently than you. Some will accept you, some won't, and that's okay. I met Dr. Judy in a meeting where I was the only one who looked like me. She didn't just welcome me; she opened doors I didn't even know existed. She introduced me to the Orange County community and nominated me for the prestigious International Women's Forum, specifically the Los Angeles chapter known as the Trusteeship. This was an invitation-only group of incredible women leaders from around the world who had achieved extraordinary things. Through Dr. Judy, I also met Michelle Jordan, who nominated me for a mentorship program sponsored by the National Organization of Women (NOW). These connections changed my life. Unity, I've learned, is about building bridges. When you meet the right people, doors can open in ways you never imagined, just like they did for me with Dr. Judy, Gloria Zigner, Barbara Taylor, and Ruth Ko. Not everyone you meet will connect with you, but some will, and those relationships can be life-changing.

T — Trustworthiness: Treating others how you want to be treated really does come full circle. When I first met Betty, I made it a point to be honest about my struggles instead of pretending everything was perfect. That honesty built a connection. When you find someone you can trust, it's a relief to be yourself around them. Trust is everything in relationships, but not everyone is trustworthy. You must be careful and choose the right people. I have been so lucky to meet some amazing women and men: Nat D. Williams, Ruth Ko, Gloria Zigner, Irene Kinoshita, Betty Lamarr, Nella Grady, Sue Parks, Joseph Lee, Betty Mower, Vance Caesar, Barbara Taylor, Dr. Judy Rosner, and Michelle Jordan. They were all so supportive because we had that mutual trust. I could be myself with them, and they felt comfortable with me too. That's the power of being genuine; it creates real, lasting connections.

S — Spirituality: I love the scripture that calls us to "love your neighbor as yourself." It reminds me that loving others begins with loving yourself—because if you don't value yourself, it's hard to truly love anyone else. Love is the foundation of my faith. In heaven, there will be no race, no segregation, no discrimination, and no prejudice. God created us all equal, and I believe He loves us all and commands us to love one another. That's why being the only Black woman at an event has never defined my experience. At our core, we share the same human essentials: we bleed the same red blood, breathe the same air, share the same internal structure, and we all live and one day will die. So it shouldn't matter whether someone is Black or White. What matters is love. God is love—and if you love God, you should love your neighbor as yourself.

CHAPTER 12

Juggling: The Art of Balance

Life balance is not about being perfect, it's about knowing that success and personal happiness go together. Surround yourself with supportive people, focus on gratitude, and stick to what really matters to you.

It was around 6 p.m. on a Wednesday, and I was at Chapman University rehearsing for CHOC Follies. Gloria Zigner, also known as Ms. Society for Orange County, was in charge of raising funds for Children's Hospital of Orange County (CHOC). She'd dedicated more than twenty years to this cause, raising millions before she passed away.

This was either the second or third CHOC Follies, and I volunteered as a singer and dancer for the event. After finishing up a dance rehearsal, I walked over to an empty row of seats in the old theatre where we were practicing. As I sat down, I noticed an older gentleman sitting at the end of the row. He had a distinguished look about him. I nodded and greeted him with a quick, "Good evening," before settling a few seats away.

While I watched the rehearsal, Gloria came over and said, "Martha, come here. I want you to meet a good friend of mine, Vance Caesar." As it turned out, this was the gentleman I had greeted earlier. I walked over, and Vance stood up to shake my hand. He was tall and striking. He asked me to sit down, so I did, leaving one seat between us. Gloria left to chat with someone else, and Vance turned to me and asked, "So, why are you volunteering for the CHOC Follies?"

I laughed and said, "It's hard to say no to Gloria."

He smiled and replied, "Yes, she's passionate about this event, and for good reason."

We continued talking, and he asked me more questions, which I answered politely. Then, he hit me with, "So, how do you make your living?"

That got me going. I lit up with excitement and shared some details about how I started IMRI, what we do, the types of customers we serve, and the results we have achieved over the years. To say I was exhilarated to share my success with him would be an understatement.

Eventually, he asked me if I had children. I smiled and said, "Yes, three boys, a girl, and my husband's five children living in St. Lucia, making up a blended family of nine children." Adrian was 25 by then, Maronya was 17, and Raymond was 10. Daniel's son, Bradley, 11, was the only one living with us at that time. Somehow, the conversation circled back from my children and family to IMRI again, and I kept talking enthusiastically, with him listening attentively.

He then asked a question I wasn't expecting.

"How often do you get to spend time with your children?"

That one hit me. I paused. It was not an easy question to answer because, honestly, I was working so much and always away from them that I didn't get to spend as much time with them as I wanted. Now, here I was adding something else to my plate that kept me away.

I looked at him with tears in my eyes and said softly, "Not as much as I want to . . . or as much as I should."

He looked straight into my eyes, and said, "We've talked so much about your business, and I can see how excited you are about it. But when you talk about your children, I sense sadness." He then asked, "Do you feel guilty about the time you get to spend with your family?"

That question caught me off guard. I didn't even know this guy, and suddenly, I was crying and getting emotional. I got up to leave, but he stopped me and said, "You know, you can fix this. I help people with balancing life for a living, and I've worked with busy executives like you who are struggling with what you are experiencing."

He reached in his pocket and presented me with his business card. "Take my card. If you ever want to talk, let's grab lunch and talk about this."

As I wiped my tears, I took his card. The way he looked at me—with so much compassion—I could tell he was a good person, someone spiritual and kind. I left and rushed to the restroom, my mind racing. I tucked the card into my purse, knowing I would take him up on that lunch invitation. But I felt torn. Vance had seen me light up when I talked about IMRI but barely show any joy when I mentioned my children. The guilt hit me hard. I love my children so much, but I had to admit that I was not spending enough time with them, and it was starting to weigh on me. When I went back to the rehearsal, I noticed Vance was gone, and a strange sadness lingered within me.

The next day, I called him. We set up lunch, and that conversation led to something much bigger, an agreement for him to become my personal coach. As my coach, Vance was also a mentor, guiding me through the ups and downs of leadership. He pointed out something I hadn't realized: I had completely lost myself while chasing my dreams. It was a hard truth to face, but he helped me put the pieces back together. With his guidance, I finally found balance in my life and let go of the constant guilt I had been carrying.

At the time, I felt like I was losing control of everything. The demands of the business and my drive to achieve my goals were pulling me away from what mattered most. I would lose the balance between building IMRI and being present for my family, especially my children. Maronya was in high school, and our bond had been established, but Raymond and Bradley were still in elementary school. Bradley and Raymond were active in sports; both boys played Pop Warner football and baseball. Raymond often asked for more of my time and would get upset anytime I had to travel.

Even when I wasn't traveling, I would stay late at the office or get caught up in evening events, which meant I missed out on dinners, games, and school events. Even when I was at home most weekends, I worked a lot. Bradley and Raymond loved when I was there, and I could feel the impact of my absence on them. I felt so guilty but didn't know how to fix it.

Once, after traveling back and forth between cities on business for two weeks, I was late picking up Raymond from an after-school activity. I had been juggling so much and lost track of time. When I finally got there, he was sitting outside alone, waiting for me. As he got in the car, he said, "Mama, do you always have to be late? It's bad you missed the match. You could at least pick me up on time." His words cut deep, and I broke down.

"Baby, Mama is so sorry," I said. "The traffic was awful, and I couldn't control it."

He looked at me and said, "Any excuse. You just don't care."

Hearing that shattered my heart. I cried the whole way home. I could see how disappointed he was, and it stayed with me. That moment was my wake-up call. Something had to change.

According to Vance's description, I was living three intertwined roles: wife, mother, and entrepreneur. Through his guidance, I gradually learned how to balance these aspects of my identity, rediscovering what it means to feel whole again. Starting a business throws your life out of balance; that's the nature of it. The demands are intense. Priorities shift. Even with the best plans, the impact on your time, your family, your marriage, and your inner peace can be huge. Sacrifices are inevitable. But as Dolly Parton once said, "The way I see it, if you want the rainbow, you gotta put up with the rain." That said, there are ways to face the rain and still find your rainbow without getting completely soaked.

Vance once pointed out something that hit me hard: "Martha Daniel" had become "IMRI." When people asked me about myself, all

I talked about was my company. It was obvious to him that I had lost my identity. I had become my business. Over time, Vance helped me realize how much IMRI had taken over my life. It had become my top priority, and there was no separation between me and my company. I was constantly chasing my goals, and it came at a huge cost: I was sacrificing my family, my children, and my happiness. I had become a slave to IMRI, letting my dream take over everything.

Through it all, Daniel was a rock. He never complained, even when I felt guilty for how much I was away. He'd always encourage me, saying, "It won't be like this forever. You need to do what you need to do." Honestly, I could not have asked for a better husband during that time. He didn't mind cooking, taking care of the children, doing chores, housekeeping, and even handling paying the bills. Daniel is my blessing, no doubt about it. But I still felt guilty every time he dropped me off at the airport for trips that sometimes lasted a week.

Even though Daniel was working evenings at the Montage Hotel, he still managed to keep everything at home running smoothly with Raymond and Bradley. He was the stricter, more by-the-book parent, sometimes too much so for the boys. That's why they always wanted me around. When I was home, I brought more balance, loosened up some of the rules, and we had fun together, but not enough because of my schedule.

Raymond spent two weeks a month with his dad, Ron, who gave us a little breathing room. But Raymond and I were so close that it was hard for us to be apart. Every time I hugged and kissed him goodbye before heading to the airport, he'd tear up and ask, "Mama, how long will you be gone?" While I was traveling, he'd call me all the time to tell me what was going on. Without fail, he'd end the call by saying, "Mama, I miss you." Hearing that broke my heart every time.

I used to carry so much guilt about missing important moments with my children because of work. I was constantly on the go, working around the clock, and even when I was home, my mind was still stuck on IMRI. Physically, I was there, but mentally, not so much. Vance helped me see that. He taught me that I didn't have to choose between my family and my business. I needed balance. I needed to make quality time with my children and husband as much of a priority as hitting my business goals. They had to become part of my dream. Once I made that shift, I could be fully present with them when we were together. For me, it came down to balance and planning.

Vance suggested that I put everything that matters—family, children, work—on my calendar. If it was important to me, I should make time for it and rarely miss it. That small change completely changed my perspective. He also helped me realize a few key things:

1. Goals don't mean much if you don't have someone to share them with.
2. I am not only an entrepreneur, I am also a mom and a wife.
3. Life is not always perfectly balanced. Some roles will need more attention than others at different times, and that's okay.
4. Balance is not about splitting time equally; it's about making the time you spend meaningful.
5. Your calendar is not only for work; it should be used to prioritize family, too.

With that advice, I started scheduling family dinners a few times a week, making sure my children's events were on my calendar, and planning regular date nights with Daniel. Even a little quality time with my family helped ease the guilt and keep those relationships strong. When I was with them, I made sure to focus completely, with no distractions. I even started talking more about my family and life, and less about work, which helped me put everything in perspective.

Working with Vance was one of the best decisions I made for both my business and my personal life. Some days, I cried my eyes out during our sessions, but they helped me reclaim my identity and remember that chasing your dreams doesn't mean losing yourself or neglecting what really matters. Sure, there are demands, but it's all about setting priorities and finding balance.

Lessons in G.U.T.S.

Achieving your dreams comes with sacrifices; there is no way around them. Sometimes, when I drive past small businesses, my heart fills with compassion because I know firsthand the struggles that come with chasing a dream. As a dreamer or entrepreneur, it's important to understand that sacrifices will be part of the journey. Life balance is not about being perfect, it's about knowing that success and personal happiness go together. Being honest with yourself and seeking help when you need it is so important. It all came together for me with G.U.T.S.

G – Gratitude: Meeting Vance was such a turning point for me. I can't tell you how grateful I am for his coaching—it was exactly what I needed. I was really struggling to juggle everything: my business, my family, and just life in general. I felt like I was constantly sacrificing too much, and my family was paying the price. Vance helped me see things differently. He showed me that I didn't have to choose between being a successful entrepreneur, a mom, and a wife—I could find a balance. He taught me to acknowledge that my dreams and goals were achievable without feeling guilty about taking time for myself or my family. The timing couldn't have been better. His guidance and ongoing mentorship helped me create a structured way to balance it all, and for the first time, I felt like I could breathe. I'll always be thankful for that. Vance was truly a blessing in my life, and he reminded me of something so important: chasing your dreams doesn't mean you have to lose sight of what matters most.

U – Unity: I have always believed in asking for help when you need it, and meeting Vance through my work with CHOC was life-changing. He helped me reconnect with my family and reminded me how important it is to share your dreams with the people you care about. He taught me how to find balance between my personal life, my family relationships, and my business goals, and how bringing it all together is the real key to success.

T – Trustworthiness: I knew I could trust Vance almost right away, even with some of the more personal parts of my life. That trust helped me accept his advice and try out the changes he suggested. Opening up about struggles I had been hiding for so long felt like finally having a safe space to breathe.

S – Spirituality: I truly believe God sends the right people into your life at the right time. Vance was exactly that for me, a spiritual blessing who showed up when I needed him most. Thanks to his coaching, I have found more peace and joy, and a stronger connection with my family, all while chasing my dreams. I'll always be grateful for everything he has taught me.

CHAPTER 13

Hire the Right Team to Bridge the Dream

Learning from the past and reflecting on lessons is an essential part of personal and professional growth. Every experience, whether a triumph or a setback, carries valuable insights that can guide future decisions and actions.

Who defines your success? I decided long ago that no one gets to define my success but me. It is up to me to decide what success looks like in my life and to step out on faith, knowing that even if I hit an obstacle, there is always another way forward. That's probably the biggest lesson I have learned about setting and achieving goals.

Some incredible individuals helped me grow IMRI. Building the right corporate management team was one of my biggest challenges. The problem (if you could call it that) is that I love everybody. I would hire people because I liked them during the interview, even if their resumes didn't quite match the job requirements. I believed they could do the job based on a good vibe or a great conversation. Having done that too many times, I learned that liking someone and thinking they are capable does not always mean they are the right fit for the position or the company culture. Some people are amazing interviewees but struggle in the actual role, and it's unfair to hire someone who doesn't have the necessary skills unless you are fully committed to investing in their training.

I have made some major hiring mistakes because I let my emotions take the lead. I wanted to help people and give them a chance, but good intentions didn't always translate into good hiring decisions. After a string of bad hires, I reached out to my friend Irene Kinoshita, a fellow entrepreneur, for advice.

"If I had all the money I've lost from hiring the wrong people, I could probably buy a whole block in Beverly Hills!" I joked. Irene laughed but quickly pointed out that what I really needed was a proper hiring process.

Over lunch, she shared a strategy that completely changed the way I approach hiring. Her sister had developed a process for her that worked and took the emotions out of the hiring process. The key was to follow the process. After thinking about our conversation, I did the same for my team.

Irene's advice taught me a valuable lesson: A thorough, objective hiring process is essential for finding the right people. Even with the new process in place, I admit I still struggled at times. Occasionally, I let my emotions creep back in or I skipped steps, and every time I did, the hire turned out to be a poor fit. After a few more failures in hiring management and corporate staff, I realized that I needed to do something different. It was time to bring in an expert in human resources, contracts and other areas, and I knew just the person.

Maronya, now 31, had been practicing employment and labor law in New York City for about three years at Morgan, Lewis & Bockius, and had decided that she didn't want to work at a big law firm anymore. We initially hired her to be General Counsel and SVP of Business Development, doing sales for the company in D.C. with the understanding that we would eventually move her to Chief Operating Officer.

She was dual hatted—managing two different roles and corresponding responsibilities at the same time—and we benefited from her knowledge when we hired for our corporate team. Maronya excelled at the sales position, bringing in a $21 million contract, closing several other contracts in the capital region, and opening many large subcontracting opportunities with large integrators. She was a force to reckon with. With no technical knowledge, she drove business to our company better than many of the experienced salespeople who ever worked for IMRI.

One day, she sat me down and said, "Mom, we need to make sure people meet specific skill and personality requirements to succeed at IMRI. Not everyone is a good fit here, and it's better to figure that out upfront than invest time and money only for them to leave after a year." Maronya's leadership in handling our HR, contracts, and back-office needs was a game-changer for IMRI.

Success is about having a vision and building the right team to help bring that vision to life. Sometimes, that means stepping back, letting go of emotions, and trusting the process. Maronya put in a great process that we continue to use today.

Expanding into the Federal Government

Breaking into the Department of Defense (DoD) was no small task. I needed to bring in people who understood government contracts and the level of security needed to win and execute those projects. That's when I hired retired military officers like Colonel Doug Bennett, Colonel Antoinette (Toni) Green, and Colonel Joe Young. They joined our team after retiring from distinguished military careers, each bringing more than twenty years of experience and leadership expertise.

Even though they were experts in their previous roles, stepping into the world of selling services and managing contracts was a whole new ball game for them. They learned a lot during their time with us, and eventually moved on to senior leadership roles at bigger companies.

Hiring the Right Corporate Partner

One day, I got a call from General Albert Edmonds's office. Small companies like mine don't usually get calls from a general's office, so I was both shocked and nervous. General Edmonds wanted to know whether IMRI was an 8(a) company and when I said yes, he explained that he wanted me to hire Brenda Taylor as a consultant under IMRI so she could complete a project for DISA, the Defense Department's IT and communications arm.

He added, "She'll tell you her rate, mark it up, but she needs to start right away."

I thanked him and got the paperwork moving. A few months after Brenda started working with us, she gave me some news that stopped me in my tracks.

"Do you know the job I'm doing for DISA will put you out of business?" she said.

I choked. "What do you mean?"

Brenda explained that the work she was doing involved consolidating the DISA DECCs, or Defense Enterprise Computing Centers. These large data centers were located around the nation, and the consolidation would leave only three computing centers open—and all the ones where IMRI had contracts were being shut down. I was in shock.

"When is this happening?" I asked, and she told me it would happen within a few months.

Panic set in, because at the time, those contracts were the only federal work we had. It was a huge wake-up call, and it taught me how quickly things can change in business, especially when government contracts are a significant part of your business. That experience—and Brenda—helped me see the bigger picture and prepare for what was next.

Later, I asked her to respond to proposals and introduce IMRI to her networks for two months after her contract ended. She agreed, and now, twenty-three years later, she's still by my side, working as IMRI's

EVP, business development and delivery and chief technology officer of the company.

When I first hired Brenda, I told her I couldn't pay her much at the time, but that one day, I would make her a millionaire. I am thrilled to have delivered on that promise. Brenda is, hands down, one of the smartest people I have ever met. She is a technical genius and a sharp businessperson. We have faced many challenges together over the years and made many great memories. She is not only an incredible partner in the business, but also my friend, someone I can always count on. She is honest, wise, deeply spiritual, and truly my sister from another mother.

Brenda has a favorite scripture she reminds me of when things get tough or when my stress levels hit the roof and my voice starts to escalate. She calmly says, "Remember, Martha, 'And we know that for those who Love God, all things work together for good, for those who are called according to His purpose.'"

Brenda's steady presence has balanced me out more times than I can count, and she has saved IMRI a few times when my fiery personality caused a hiccup or two. Over the years, we have joked about our dynamic duo personas. Sometimes we are like Huntley-Brinkley news anchors, feeding off each other perfectly. Other times, we are Lucy and Ethel, with Brenda giving me a look and saying, "Okay, Lucy, you need to stop." We have been through so much together, and we have always found a way to make a situation work.

As the primary marketing team, we have traveled coast to coast and delivered more than $400 million in contractual engagements since teaming up. Brenda could sell IT services to people at the highest levels, but she could also break tasks down for engineers and technical teams. She was always calm when closing a deal, while I would bring the passion and energy to reel people in. What makes our relationship so special is that it's professional and we are friends. Having a business partner who truly has your back and supports your dream is something every founder needs. I am lucky to have found that in Brenda. She embodies G.U.T.S.

Reflections on Challenges, Accomplishments, and Taking the Dream Further

It's hard to believe that IMRI has been in business for thirty-three years now. Over the years, we have launched three other companies, Ataraxis, E2Metron, and Cytellix. With more than $400 million in contract awards under our belts, we have had the opportunity to hire a few great hires and make some meaningful contributions in technology innovation and national projects, including the following:

Cybersecurity - 2008

In 2008, cybersecurity was beginning to dominate conversations across government and industry. That's when IMRI partnered with Lumeta Software to take on the growing need for stronger security solutions. But what set that opportunity in motion wasn't technology—it was people.

Valerie Clayton, Lumeta's federal director of business development, had worked with us before and remembered how responsive Brenda had been. That positive connection brought us back together and gave IMRI the chance to gain valuable experience in cybersecurity. Brenda and Valerie teamed up to roll out Lumeta's solutions across the Department of Defense, including DISA, the Office of the Secretary of Defense, the U.S. Army, and various intelligence agencies. Their hard work paid off and our revenues jumped from $8 million to $18 million.

Those were exciting times for IMRI and the perfect opportunity to start building the dream of Cytellix.

The Birth of Cytellix

In 2014, Brenda and I officially co-founded Cytellix, driven by the belief that cybersecurity would eventually require formal standardization, like ISO standards. This vision aligned perfectly with the work being done by National Institute of Standards and Technology (NIST).

Our early efforts did not quite pan out, but then, in September 2016, we conducted a national search and brought on Brian Berger. Brian assembled an incredible team, including Howard Lin, our chief architect. Together, they developed technical vision and built an AI platform that has earned Cytellix seven patents for innovation.

Growing Cytellix has been anything but easy. From the beginning, the company was undercapitalized. IMRI invested in it through development and now through the rollout, which has been incredibly draining for the company and for me personally. We entered the market early, but when the Department of Defense delayed the mandatory implementation of the Cybersecurity Maturity Model Certification (CMMC), it gave our competitors time to catch up.

Then came COVID. Surviving that period and holding on to the business left us in a terrible financial position. To boost sales, we brought on a new CEO. Unfortunately, that decision turned out to be a major setback. Instead of moving forward, we lost revenue and took on a significant amount of debt. The impact was devastating for both companies. There were moments when we were dangerously close to shutting down. That's when I made the decision to bring in a turnaround company, Kyma Capital, led by President Brian Brick. They helped us navigate the legal and financial challenges while we worked strategically to increase revenue. It required a significant financial investment from IMRI and from me personally, but I believed in our vision. I was determined not to give up, no matter how tough the fight became.

My faith in God carried me through. I give Him all the credit for keeping me going and for sending the right people at the right time to help me weather this storm. Every time an obstacle came up, God provided a way for me to overcome it and keep moving forward. We are not out of the woods yet, but I am so grateful I didn't give up. By keeping faith, believing in the impossible, and pushing forward with G.U.T.S., we are making progress.

Cytellix was not my first major setback. Setbacks have a funny way of showing up at the most unexpected times in life. How you handle them determines whether you overcome or succumb. You always have those two choices. Let me share a personal story to show you what I mean.

Back in 2004, I started a company called Ataraxis LLC. I had an incredible executive team, and we were on a mission to solve a big problem: helping small businesses, consumers, and public institutions protect their PCs from the growing wave of threats to their data. At the time, there was a huge gap in the market for unmanaged and unsupported PCs, and we were determined to fill it. Things looked promising. One of the big turning points came when Pete Papas, a former IT manager at Farmers Insurance, introduced us to an amazing opportunity. Pete had teamed up with a brilliant chief architect who had developed a software platform that automated software patches for laptops. We even struck a deal with Dell to provide this solution for their customer, Wellpoint, for all their physicians. We were so close, development was nearly done, and we were ready to roll it out.

And then, out of nowhere, Microsoft dropped a bombshell. They announced automated patching of their software for free. Just like that, our entire business model was finished. I had to liquidate my personal assets to cover the financial debt we'd taken on to develop and run Ataraxis. That was one of the hardest moments of my life. I remember praying to God, asking for His help to get me through such a tough time. It felt like pure despair, but my faith became my anchor and carried me through that valley. It was a two-year journey, one where my faith was tested in ways I never imagined.

That experience taught me to not let fear paralyze you, even when it feels like your world is crumbling. We had a solid business plan, but we didn't know Microsoft was working on the exact same solution. If we had done more thorough market research, digging into Gartner reports and analyzing Microsoft's strategic plans, we could have seen it coming.

When Ataraxis had to close, it was devastating. But I learned how to handle a major business setback. The first step is to accept what happened. Don't waste time dwelling on the "what ifs." Instead, focus on creating a recovery plan. Break the problem down into smaller, manageable pieces. Think about the impact on every part of your business—your employees, cash flow, customers—and prioritize what needs attention first.

Do not go alone. Turn to your resources and your network. Talk to people who've been through similar challenges. There is no shame in asking for advice. You are not the first person to face a setback, and you won't be the last. Lean on your trusted network and ask, "How would you handle this?"

One of the biggest takeaways for me was this: Failure does not mean you have failed as a person. If something doesn't go as planned, whether it's a project, a dream, or a business venture, you can still grow from it. Learn from what happened and let it reshape you into a better leader, entrepreneur, or businessperson. Every setback has a lesson, but you must be willing to look for it.

Lessons in G.U.T.S.

It's fine to look back and reflect, because after all, that's how we learn. But the goal is to gain insight so you can move forward with new strategies and adjustments to keep chasing your dream. Challenges and setbacks will come, and that's when most people feel like giving up. Don't do it! It takes G.U.T.S. to keep going and never give up.

G — Gratitude: Gratitude is everything when it comes to the people who commit to your vision. I cannot emphasize enough how thankful I am for the pioneering women who believed in me and saw my potential. They gave their time, support, friendship, and love, often making personal and professional sacrifices because they cared deeply about the company and about me. When someone adopts your dream as their own and shows unwavering loyalty, it's important to give back with fair compensation, equity, stock options, or thoughtful gifts. Always remember to give back to those who give so much to you.

I am also incredibly grateful I didn't give up after what happened with Ataraxis. That was a huge setback for IMRI and Ataraxis, as well as for my personal life. But I didn't let it stop me. Instead, I came out stronger, with a bigger net worth than I had before. That experience taught me so much about taking risks and gave me the courage to start Cytellix with a clearer understanding of what to expect. Every business comes with its own challenges. Even though IMRI initially funded Cytellix, we needed extra capital to keep growing, and there have been setbacks. But thanks to what I learned from Ataraxis, we were able to navigate the COVID crisis with investment funds. I am so thankful I didn't let those setbacks paralyze me from achieving my dream.

U — Unity: No one achieves success alone, and IMRI's journey is a testament to the dedicated individuals who helped build it. Brenda Taylor was the glue that held our company together. Her loyalty and dedication far exceeded any expectation, evolving from employee to friend and partner. We often said that if I was Moses, she was my Aaron; her skills complemented and elevated my own. We were so aligned that we could finish each other's sentences, sharing hardships, victories, spiritual growth, and a drive for continual innovation. Brenda was also instrumental in recruiting my daughter, Maronya, who brought her own remarkable skills and steadfast loyalty to the business and its mission.

This foundation of unity was strengthened by others who gave decades of service. My niece, Monica, served as our recruiter for over 25 years, ensuring we never lost a project for lack of top-tier talent. Similarly, Janet Miller gave more than 20 years of dedicated service. Like an octopus with many arms, she took on whatever role was needed, from contracts and proposal manager to office manager. These women worked in unity, supporting one another through every up and down. Their contributions highlight a core truth: building a successful organization means creating a team that is fully aligned with the mission, where every person plays a meaningful role in achieving shared goals.

T — Trustworthiness: Trust is not handed out, it's earned. I have been fortunate to work with people like Martine, Barbara, and Brenda, whose honesty and integrity matched my own. Our mutual trust laid the foundation for loyalty, and even now, I know I can call on them, and they'd answer without hesitation. That level of trust is built through consistent actions and shared values. Their dedication and loyalty have inspired me time and time again, reminding me how important trust is in any relationship.

Surrounding yourself with honest people reflects on your character as a leader and impacts your company's reputation. Honesty and trustworthiness are essential. Loyalty comes when people know they can trust you, so never take advantage of your employees, business partners, or customers. Always do the right thing. After thirty-three years in business, I can confidently say our reputation remains strong because we have prioritized doing right by everyone. When you prioritize being trustworthy and acting with integrity, you build trust and you also feel good about yourself and your achievements.

S — Spirituality: Brenda and I share a special connection through our faith. We are both active Christians and often pray together, attend Bible studies, and lean on each other during difficult times. Our faith has been a source of strength that carried us through some truly challenging moments. Brenda's spiritual support is like the wind beneath my wings. She constantly reminds me to let go of what I cannot control and to trust in God's plan. Having someone by your side who shares your faith is a gift. Brenda has been a constant source of spiritual strength for me and for IMRI.

When everything is going smoothly, it's easy to forget the source of your success and the wisdom that got you there. But when challenges arise, that's often when "S" for Spirituality reappears, when your thoughts and prayers for guidance become more frequent. Staying spiritually connected in every decision and seeking God's wisdom daily can give you strength during uncertain times. It helps you maintain hope and stay confident, knowing the outcome is in hands greater than yours. This perspective makes overcoming obstacles less stressful and more manageable because you trust the journey, even when it's tough.

CHAPTER 14

Deceit and Untrustworthy Individuals

Betrayals often reveal valuable lessons that teach you about trust, resilience, and the strength to move forward. These experiences can help you better understand the importance of setting boundaries, recognizing red flags, and appreciating the people who genuinely value and support you.

There will always be ups and downs in life, with some great moments, some tough ones, and everything in between. You will meet wonderful people, but you'll also cross paths with some who are not so great. That's when having G.U.T.S. can serve you best.

Over my years in business, I have only had four tough times caused by dishonest people. Interestingly, there were two common patterns in these situations. In two of them, the people were supposed to be my friends, and their betrayal blindsided me. The other two were classic con artists. Each experience taught me something valuable.

When Someone Tries to Steal Your Business

One of the hardest betrayals I ever experienced still stings to this day. It came from someone I trusted deeply, my mentor, of all people. I had brought Matt into my company as president, thinking his years of experience would help us grow. But it turned out he had a completely different agenda.

After reviewing our financial accounts, he started deliberately increasing expenses. At first, I didn't understand why, but then it became clear that he was trying to drive the company into bankruptcy so he could buy it out and take it over. He had convinced himself that taking over my company was easier than starting his own from scratch.

Thankfully, my CFO at the time, Chris Minoudis, wasn't about to let that happen. I'll never forget a Monday morning during our finance meeting when Matt was pushing us to approve an outrageously expensive purchase. Chris suddenly stood up, slammed his fist on the table, and shouted, "I will not watch you bankrupt her business!" His voice was shaking with anger as he continued, "You are wrong for this. You are deliberately trying to destroy this company, and I won't stand for it." Then, he stormed out of the room, slamming the door behind him.

Matt just sat there, stunned, and then turned to me and said, "I refuse to be yelled at like that. I am going to fire him."

That was it for me. I stood up and said, "No, you will not." I left the room and went straight to Chris's office.

Chris was fuming.

"Martha," he said, "he's trying to put you out of business. This guy is awful, and I can't watch him do this to you."

I was already upset with Matt for so many reasons, but hearing Chris say it out loud made it real. He looked me in the eye and said, "You have got to get him out of here."

I nodded and said, "I'll do just that."

I went back to my office, shaking, and called Vance. I was crying when he picked up.

"Vance," I said, "Matt is trying to put me out of business, and Chris says I need to fire him."

Vance paused.

"I already know," he said. "Are you ready to do it?"

I hesitated and finally said, "Yes, but I don't think I can do it alone. We've worked together for so many years, and even though I know he's been doing wrong, I don't think I can look him in the eye and fire him."

Vance didn't miss a beat. "I'll come over and do it. I'll be there in an hour."

Those minutes waiting for Vance felt like an eternity. I sat at my desk, crying, asking myself repeatedly, *Why is he doing this to me? Why? I trusted him.*

When Vance arrived, he came into my office and reassured me, "It's going to be okay." Then he went to Chris's office, and finally, into Matt's. It felt like forever, but it was only about fifteen minutes before Vance came back and said, "He's leaving. I asked him to pack up his things." Within ten minutes, Matt walked out of the office for good. Vance gave me a hug and said, "This is a good thing. I'll send you a draft letter for his termination."

I was devastated. This was someone I had known for eighteen years. Not only had he tried to destroy my business, but he had also betrayed me on a deep personal level. And as if that were not enough, he filed a lawsuit against us for his salary and bonus, knowing full well we were struggling financially. We paid him immediately and it felt like pouring salt in the wound.

Through it all, I know God was watching over me. Shortly after this betrayal, we landed a major contract that helped us recover financially. About a year later, I heard that Matt had been hired as COO by another woman-owned company nearby. Tragically, he pulled the same stunt, bankrupted her business, and bought it for himself.

That experience was one of the most challenging I have ever endured. It taught me invaluable lessons about trust, leadership, and the strength it takes to stand firm when everything is working against you.

Lesson Learned: Always stay hands-on with your business, especially when it comes to finances. Even if you trust someone completely, don't hand over full financial control. Make sure you are reviewing and approving a solid business plan with a clear budget before anything gets rolling. And when it comes to spending, contracts, or signing checks, you should always have the final say. Whoever's managing your finances should report directly to you, no exceptions. This way, you'll avoid any surprises. Above all, stay on top of your business outcomes and never delegate your leadership responsibilities entirely, even if it's to a friend, family member, or your CPA. It's your business, so own it!

Stealing from Your Mentor

After Hurricane Katrina devastated New Orleans, my mentor, Lurita Doan, reached out to me with a request. She wanted me to help a young entrepreneur who had been deeply impacted by the storm start her IT business. My mentee was young, ambitious, and driven. She had a master's degree and a true entrepreneurial spirit. Before Katrina, she had run a small ice cream shop, but the storm forced her to shut it down.

When I met my mentee, I saw her potential immediately. We brought her into our company, giving her access to our policies, procedures, and everything she needed to establish her business. I personally mentored her, and Brenda and I worked closely with her, teaching her how to write proposals, develop marketing strategies, and sharpen her sales skills. Watching her grow and embrace our guidance was incredibly rewarding. Brenda and I even traveled with her for sales calls, gave her access to our systems, and covered all the expenses.

When we graduated from the Small Business Administration's 8(a) Stars program, we worked with our contracting officers to transfer contracts to her company. Her business ended up taking fifty-one percent of the contracts, while IMRI retained forty-nine percent.

For the first year, everything seemed fine. But then, greed took over her. As the prime contractor, my mentee had direct access to the contracting officer. She used that access to renegotiate our $3 million contract behind our backs, cutting us out completely. We didn't even realize something was wrong until we followed up with the interim contracting officer about the renewal, only to find out it wasn't happening. When we called my mentee, she never mentioned that the contract had been moved under another agreement, excluding us entirely. It wasn't until the original contracting officer returned from maternity leave that we learned my mentee had entered a new contract without us. We were blindsided.

Brenda called my mentee to ask what had happened. My mentee's response? "Your contract ended, and they didn't renew it. I started another contract, and I don't need a subcontractor on this one." Brenda pressed her, asking about the scope of the work, and my mentee admitted, "It's similar, but I don't need IMRI's help with it."

Brenda called me, furious.

"She took our contract and cut us out of the work."

I called my mentee and asked her about the contract.

"I needed the money, and your contract wasn't being renewed, so they gave me the contract," she said.

I paused, trying to stay calm, and asked, "Why didn't you discuss this with us?"

She replied, "I didn't need to because this contract is mine. I didn't do anything wrong."

My heart raced as I took a deep breath.

"I taught you a lot of things," I said, "but I never taught you to steal from anyone."

I continued, "We gave you millions in work, you made a significant profit, and then you went behind our backs and took the renewed contract. And you still don't think you did anything wrong?" I was getting angrier and added, "You didn't even include us in any of the work or share any revenue from the new contract. After everything I have done for you, I can't believe you'd do this to me! It's a small world, and one day you'll look back on this and regret it."

I was heartbroken. This betrayal cut me to the core because we had poured so much into helping her grow her business. I supported her selflessly. She was not only a mentee to me, she was like a daughter.

Brenda and I had stayed at her home, supported her through her breast cancer journey, and offered her spiritual guidance. Seeing her disregard all of that was devastating.

We had transitioned two of our 8(a) contracts to her company because we could no longer serve as the prime. She agreed to subcontract 49% of the revenue to us in return. However, when the contracts came up for renewal, she retained 100% of the $3 million contract. Even after this, she tried to take the other contract the following year. Thankfully, the contracting officer reached out to us and ensured we were included.

Lessons Learned: Trust is crucial, but you must have contracts that cover you in case things go south. Betrayal can shake your faith in people, and it's hard to open up again after being burned. But don't let one bad experience close you off completely. Trusting again takes time, and it's okay to be cautious. Not everyone is out to take advantage of you. Most people are good and worth believing in. Just make sure you are legally protected so you can trust with confidence, not fear.

Beware of Con Artists

I met Dawn at a Navy event in San Diego. She was a business development manager for a big-name government contractor, had fifteen years of experience, and came across as super professional. I introduced her to Brenda, and we all hit it off. During our conversation, Dawn mentioned she was planning to leave her current job to start her own business. She even had a contracting vehicle and offered to let us use it until we got our own. It sounded like a great deal.

Not long after, a contracting opportunity popped up that we knew we could win. Brenda called Dawn and said, "Hey, we've got a Navy opportunity. It's worth about $3 million. What do you think?"

Dawn jumped on it immediately. "Yes, let's bid on it together," she said.

The idea was that her company would be the prime contractor, and IMRI would subcontract since we didn't have the contracting vehicle to bid on our own. Later that day, Brenda called her to iron out the deal. We would write the proposal and give her fifty-one percent of the contract if we won.

Dawn seemed casual about it.

"Sounds fair, but I am not looking for much. Maybe just one position. I just want to help you all break into the Navy in San Diego," she said.

Brenda said, "We'll give you more than one position. Honestly, we can even split it fifty/fifty if that works for you."

It seemed fair since her company was not up and running yet. It was a business on paper only. We figured she didn't want to deal with payroll or the day-to-day operations because she was still working for a big company. We won the contract, and things were going great. We set up new offices in D.C., hired staff, bought furniture, laptops, everything you'd need to run an operation with twelve employees. For three months, it was smooth sailing. Then, out of nowhere, Dawn called me on a Friday afternoon and dropped a bombshell.

"I sold the company," she said. "The new owners will contact you."

I was stunned. "What does this mean for our contract?" I asked.

She brushed me off. "I have to go. They'll explain everything."

It turned out her company was only a shell, and this contract was her first and only win. Even though it felt a bit off at the start, we moved forward, trusting her word. The new owners emailed us and invited us to meet them in Washington, D.C. Brenda and I made the trip, not sure what we were walking into. We met the new guy at the City Club downtown. He was tall, slim, and gave off used car salesperson vibes. From the moment we sat down, he got straight to the point.

Leaning back in his chair, he said, "Let's make this short and sweet. I am taking over the contract, and I don't need your company's help." Instantly, the rug was pulled out from under us.

I was in shock. "Are you serious?"

He smirked. "By the time you try to fight this in court, the contract will be over, and I'll file bankruptcy on the company. You'd be wasting your money."

Brenda jumped in. "What about our employees?"

That same smug smirk. "Oh, we already told them they'll be working for us now. We don't need anything from you. We have our own office, furniture, equipment, and now . . . your employees."

I was speechless. I stood up, looked at Brenda, and said, "Let's go." As we walked out, I could barely think straight.

When we got back to the hotel, I called Dawn immediately. She picked up, and I went straight in. "What the hell was that?"

Her response? "I sold the company. It's not mine anymore. I can't make decisions about it."

I was livid. "You know this could ruin us. Can't you do anything?"

She was so calm it was chilling. "I don't control what they do."

I was shaking with frustration. "You know what? I am covered by the blood. Nothing you do will hurt me. I'll get through this. Goodbye."

That whole ordeal was a gut punch to our business. It almost drove us into bankruptcy. Dawn completely ghosted us after that. Somehow, we managed to get enough money to cover payroll. But the bills kept piling up, and we barely stayed afloat. Then, out of nowhere, I got a call from the Navy in Stennis, Mississippi. They wanted to sole-source IMRI a $3 million contract and needed us to start immediately. That call came at the right time, like a blessing we didn't see coming.

Lessons Learned: Be careful who you partner with in business. Take the time to thoroughly vet them before diving in. There are a lot of con artists out there. You won't always see them coming, but you can protect yourself by doing your homework and setting clear terms upfront. At the time, we didn't have the resources to fight them in court, especially out of state. It was a hard lesson, but one we'll never forget. Stay vigilant and always remember that not everyone plays fair.

Don't Trust Every Referral

When we met John from an Engineering Firm in northern California, he came across as a kind, grandfatherly guy. He showed Brenda and me a little gadget, a submeter, that connects to a building's electrical meter to break down billing for each unit. It sounded revolutionary, especially for government and commercial buildings. He even claimed Google had already rolled it out in other countries. According to him, it needed a small tweak to work in the U.S., and the Department of Energy had a program to make it happen. Everything he said sounded totally legit.

We met him for lunch in Santa Cruz, where he pulled out the submeter and said, "This is going to revolutionize the industry and make a huge difference in commercial and government buildings."

I am not the engineering type, but I listened while Brenda dove in with a bunch of technical questions.

John explained, "I need a little more funding to finish the last phase, and the federal government is going to jump on this technology." He even offered us exclusive rights to sell it to the federal government at a special price once it was ready.

We did our homework. His claims seemed solid, so we decided to move forward.

We signed an agreement with John and gave him money for the first batch, which he said would be ready in five months. Meanwhile, we hired an engineer, set up everything we'd need to sell this equipment to the government, and even named the product "E2Metron." We were convinced this was going to bring IMRI recognition and revenue like never before. But then, things got weird.

After five months, John called and said, "We're waiting on parts from China, so it'll be another three months." Fine, delays happen. Our engineer even visited his offices and saw an updated version of the meter, which seemed impressive. We were still optimistic.

Another six months went by, and John called again. This time he said, "We need $400,000 for special equipment to properly test the meter." At this point, red flags were flying everywhere. Over a year had passed, and we still didn't have a finished product.

We decided to check out his facilities in Santa Cruz. What we saw was . . . fake. Our engineers, who attended the demonstrations, spotted flaws right away. They challenged the design, questioned the test results, and ultimately concluded the whole thing was staged. It was a sham. They told us there wasn't even a real product. We'd already lost $250,000, and it turned out we were not the only ones. John had also convinced another investor to give him $1.5 million for a similar project in Mexico, which (surprise, surprise) he did not deliver on either.

In the end, John walked away with our money and other people's money too. No patents, no product, only empty promises. If he had developed the submeter, we all could've made millions. But instead, his lies ruined the opportunity for everyone.

Lessons Learned: We really messed up on this deal. Handing over money upfront without clear milestones? A big mistake. We should have tied payments to actual progress and pay when a milestone had been delivered. We didn't fact-check his claims about the submeter being used elsewhere. We trusted him because, well, he seemed kind and trustworthy. Sometimes the nicest people can be the most deceptive. Verify everything. Build trust slowly. Pay in stages based on real results. Protect yourself and your investment to make sure you don't end up burned, like we did.

The Great Deal

Sometimes, chasing success can make you lose sight of what really matters. When money's tight or the pressure to succeed feels overwhelming, it can be tempting to cut corners, bend the rules, or agree to something that doesn't sit right with you. But success is never worth sacrificing your integrity. Wrong is wrong, no matter how you try to spin it.

After a major financial setback in my business, I hired a retired U.S. Army colonel who brought me what he called an amazing opportunity. Honestly, it sounded too good to be true and, as it turned out, it was. He had come up with a way to make the opportunity look legit, but deep down, it was unethical.

The deal involved collaborating with another colonel, someone still on active duty and in charge of awarding contracts. The plan was to set up a way to compensate him in a way that was "semi-legal" (his words, not mine). He estimated we could make over $25 million, maybe even more, in a few years. At first, I was tempted. Who wouldn't be when your business is struggling? But as he explained how things would work, it became crystal clear to both Brenda and me that this was shady, unethical, and absolutely not something we could do.

He kept calling, trying to convince me. I wrestled with it for days. At one point, I even called Brenda and asked, "Do you think maybe we're overlooking something? Could this actually work out for the company?"

She didn't hesitate.

"Absolutely not," she said. "This is unethical, and you know it. He knows it. It's shady. There is some gray in it, sure, but we cannot entertain this any longer."

Her conviction stuck with me, but I still couldn't shake the internal battle. Finally, I called the colonel and told him, "Look, I get it. This could bring in money, but I'm not comfortable with the risks or the way it's being done. I can't do it."

Even after that, I second-guessed myself. Business was tight, and the idea of turning down that kind of money kept creeping back into my mind. That's when I called another person that I trust deeply, my pastor, Rev. Dr. Mark Whitlock. I laid the whole thing out for him, trying (and failing) to justify why it might be okay.

He listened, then looked me in the eye and said, "Martha, you can always say no." I tried to explain more, but he cut me off and repeated, "Martha, you can always say no."

That's when it hit me. No matter how tempting the deal was or how I tried to justify it, it was wrong, plain and simple. I told Pastor Mark he was right, and I stuck to my decision.

The colonel only worked for us for about nine months. After not accepting that deal, we decided to part ways. Not long after, he started his own company, and we heard he was growing fast. Brenda and I figured he probably went ahead with the deal on his own. Twelve years later, we found out he and several others had been caught and sent to federal prison. If we'd gone through with that deal, we would've been caught in the same scheme and likely ended up in prison too. Thank God we stayed true to our morals and kept our integrity intact, even when the pressure was on. Tragically, the colonel passed away while serving his five-year sentence.

I am so grateful we said no. That one decision saved us from so much pain and regret. It's a reminder that no deal, no amount of money, is ever worth compromising your integrity.

Lessons in G.U.T.S.

It takes G.U.T.S. to handle setbacks and betrayals, and spot when someone does not have your best interests at heart. Over the years, I have learned to lean on my G.U.T.S. to make smarter decisions and to bounce back from not-so-great ones. In the end, having G.U.T.S. is about staying true to yourself, spotting red flags early, and building relationships based on mutual respect and integrity. It's not always easy, but it's worth it.

G – Gratitude: When you bring someone onto your team or give them an opportunity, it's fair to expect a bit of appreciation in return. I am thankful that most people have been trustworthy during my decades in business. Sure, there have been a few betrayals, but no legal contract can make someone honest if they have already decided not to be. Contracts help you handle breaches, but they don't guarantee integrity. What I am most grateful for is that my personal values have helped me forgive those who have wronged me, stay honest, and hold onto my integrity. The moment you spot dishonesty, it's time to cut ties.

U – Unity: Unity in relationships should be a two-way street. Not every connection needs to become a partnership, and it's important to stay discerning. Some people may approach you with hidden agendas, so take time to evaluate their character. Observe their actions, how they treat others, and the company they keep; these details can reveal a lot. Healthy relationships are built on trust, integrity, and mutual benefit. If someone's morals seem questionable, don't ignore the warning signs. I learned this the hard way with Dawn, who used a brief relationship to take advantage of my kindness. The red flags were there—her insistence that she wanted nothing and her actions outside her employer's knowledge—but I overlooked them. Networking isn't about exact reciprocity, but it does require mutual respect and appreciation. Great relationships are balanced, supportive, and never one-sided.

T – Trustworthiness: Trust isn't just about words—it's about actions. While words can create an image, actions reveal the truth. Often, it's the small, everyday behaviors that speak the loudest. Take John, for example. He came across as a warm, grandfatherly figure, soft-spoken, kind, and approachable. He shared impressive insights about his customer base and even showcased a prototype of the meter. On the surface, he seemed entirely trustworthy. But when we dug deeper into his background, other ventures, and even the person who introduced us, several red flags emerged that would have completely altered our perspective on partnering with him. Before entering any business relationship, it's crucial to do your due diligence—ask for references, conduct thorough research, and spend meaningful time with the individual. How do they treat a server at lunch? How do they behave in meetings? Do they show respect and gratitude? These seemingly small moments can offer valuable insights into their character. My experiences with John and Dawn taught me the importance of slowing down when building business relationships. Trust is built through patience, attention to detail, and a willingness to notice the subtle nuances that we often might overlook.

S —Spirituality: I initially found it difficult to move past my hurt with each situation. Sometimes, resentments linger. That's when praying to God can make a difference. When you ask God for the strength to forgive, you seek help and invite guidance, support, and peace into your life. Through prayer, you can begin to let go of that anger and bitterness, trusting that with faith, true forgiveness and healing are possible. It's not easy, but turning to God in difficult moments can help lighten the burden and restore a sense of calm within you.

CHAPTER 15

Wrapped In God's Spirit

With God at the center of your life, your foundation is strong.
His guidance give you wisdom during uncertain times, and
His love reminds you that you are never alone even when
things get tough.

My belief in God started pretty early in life, thanks to my mom. Sunday School every week was non-negotiable. I delivered my first sermon at my kindergarten graduation. I was the main speaker and performed a skit called "I Had Ten Pennies." After changing out of my white graduation dress and into black pedal pusher pants and a black-and-white top, I walked onto the stage.

There was a little log in front of me, and while holding my pennies, I had to pretend to trip over it and drop them all. The pennies scattered everywhere on the stage. I actually had to rehearse that fall a few times to make sure I didn't hurt myself. After I "fell," I started picking up the pennies one by one, telling a story about how each penny represented a blessing from God. When I got to the tenth penny, I couldn't find it; it was missing. So, I turned it into a moment about giving and shared how I would give that last penny to the Lord.

I memorized the whole skit. Ms. Collins, my kindergarten teacher, rehearsed with me every day at school, and then my mom and sister practiced with me every night at home. On the day of graduation, there were so many people in the audience who I recognized, so I wasn't nervous at all. I was used to being in front of a crowd since I was a lead singer in the children's choir at church. I glanced over at Ms. Collins during the performance, and she was smiling so big, proud of how well I was doing. I didn't miss a beat.

The applause, the standing ovation, and most of all, my mom's face warmed my heart. Mama clapped so hard and beamed with pride at my performance. Daddy was smiling too. He was not as expressive as Mama, but I could tell he was proud. That performance was a special dedication to God that set the tone for my life.

Making a Difference in the World

What will my grandchildren, other dreamers, men, women, entrepreneurs, and specifically Black Americans accomplish because of the doors I have opened and the lessons I am leaving behind in this book? That question stays with me, and it all connects to the last letter in G.U.T.S.: Spirituality. One of my favorite Bible verses is 1 Corinthians 2:9: "No eye has seen, no ear has heard, and no mind has imagined what God has prepared for those who love him." For me, it always starts with my love for God.

As a young girl, I was all about my church. By age ten, I was teaching Sunday School, and even earlier, at age five, I was singing gospel songs with my brother Jerome and our neighbor Leola. Later, I helped form the first youth choir at Alcy Road Church of Christ, working with teenagers to bring it to life. I knew my Bible well, loved teaching, and was passionate about making a difference.

But the Church of Christ had strict rules about what women could do. Women were not allowed to lead beyond teaching or working with children. Even our mixed-gender choir stirred up issues, and I caught criticism from the deacons for wearing pants to a children's rehearsal and using my piano at home to teach songs. The church didn't believe in choirs, only singing groups, and even in those groups, women were not allowed to sing during worship. Only men could lead the groups, but since no one else stepped up, I did, and that caused more friction.

Eventually, I felt so disillusioned that I stepped away. I quit leading the youth singing group and left the church for about ten years. But my love for God never wavered. During those years, I drifted in and out of different churches. About fourteen years later, I found my way back to the Church of Christ in Mission Viejo, California. The pastor there welcomed me warmly and gave me the chance to start a women's Bible study. This church was mostly White and far more liberal, which was refreshing. Although women still couldn't participate in services, they were active in other ministries. I taught Bible study, and it was clear that the women connected deeply with the lessons. It opened my eyes to the impact I could have. I always felt like God had something special planned for me, even if I didn't know exactly what it was yet.

Growing up, I had never seen a woman preacher, so becoming one was never on my radar. But in 1995, everything shifted. Joy Banks, one of my first business development managers at IMRI, invited me to visit Christ Our Redeemer (COR), an African Methodist Episcopal (AME) Church in Costa Mesa to sing with their small choir on Sundays. At the time, my family was still members of the Mission Viejo Church of Christ, so I started splitting my time between the two churches.

Eventually, I met Rev. Christilene Weaver, the pastor at COR and the first woman preacher I had ever seen. She was incredible. We got to know each other during her time at the church before she left to pursue her master's in divinity at Harvard. Meeting her planted a seed in my mind. Women could be great pastors. That realization opened a whole new world of possibilities for me. I had never considered becoming a Pastor before, but the thought crept into my mind as I watched Rev. Weaver in action.

In 2003, Daniel and I officially joined COR under Pastor Mark Whitlock's leadership. Pastor Mark was an inspiring leader. He was a businessman who had been mentored by Rev. Cecil Murray of First AME Church in Los Angeles. In 2004, I teamed up with First Lady

Hermia "Mama Mia" Shegog-Whitlock to launch COR's first women's Bible study, "Making It Real." Together, we built a ministry that's still going strong twenty years later. One of the highlights has been our annual retreat, which has become a safe space for women to grow spiritually, support each other in their careers, navigate motherhood, and strengthen their marriages. Women have opened up to share their struggles and align their lives with God's plan.

Even though I had always known I was a strong teacher of God's word, I never saw myself as a minister. Pastor Mark would often ask me, "What are you afraid of?"

I would tell him, "I'm not scared of anything." But deep down, I had my doubts. I had been journaling about feeling called to ministry, but I wasn't one hundred percent sure I could do it. Thank God for my journaling time. During those quiet, reflective moments, my soul feels most at peace, and I can truly connect with Him for guidance and reassurance. In those moments, I feel God leading me, step by step, toward the path He's laid out for me.

My Journey to Ordination as an AME Minister

In 2004, I began a five-year Ministerial Ordination Training program in the Fifth District of the AME Connectional Church. It was intense—seven months of training every year—and also incredibly rewarding. After three years, I was ordained as a local deacon, and two years later, I became a local elder. Our graduating class was the largest they'd ever had in LA, with eighteen of us completing the program. The night before graduation, we gathered for an evening of prayer, worship, sharing testimonies, and singing praise songs. It was a powerful, emotional night, one of the most transformative experiences of my life.

As the night went on, I felt a deep cleansing of my soul. I let go of guilt, unforgiveness, insecurities, anxiety, and so much more. It was like the Holy Spirit was working inside me, stripping away all those burdens, a true inner and outward experience with God. My soul became anchored in Him.

On the day of my ordination as a deacon in 2007, more than sixty friends, family, and my COR church family came to celebrate with me. It was such an exciting and emotional day. When our class marched in, the room was buzzing with energy. I was already overwhelmed, but when the bishop approached each of us individually to pray, something extraordinary happened. As he pressed my face into the Bible and placed his hand on my head, my heart pounded, and tears poured down my face. I couldn't even hear his prayer because I was so overwhelmed with the realization that I was now officially representing God. It felt like an explosion of joy inside me, like I was floating and surrounded by stars.

That moment was bigger than anything I could have imagined. Despite everything I had going on—my demanding job at IMRI, traveling, being a mom, and my responsibilities at COR—I had completed this assignment from God. Only God could have given me the strength to do it all.

Two years later, in 2010, I went through it all again when I was ordained as an elder. All those same emotions came rushing back. I reflected on the dedication and hard work it took to get there: five years of studying and completing assignments, driving to LA for meetings and services, and serving at my church. It was another reminder of what's possible when you let God guide your steps and you believe in yourself. Philippians 4:13 has always been my anchor: "I can do all things through Christ who strengthens me."

Being chosen by God to serve in ministry for more than twenty years has been my greatest accomplishment. Ministry is not easy. Representing God and leading others is a huge responsibility. Trusting Him to work through my obedience has brought peace that surpasses all understanding. It's been an incredible journey, and I am so grateful for every step along the way.

It has been an honor to be the first female minister ordained at COR and the second ordination under Pastor Mark Whitlock's leadership. When I told my husband back in 2004 that God had called me, I wasn't sure what he thought, but I was certain he would support me because God has always been the foundation of our lives. After my ordination, Daniel became a chaplain for the jail ministry at COR, an usher, and has been incredibly active in so many ways.

Putting God first has always been central to my life because I believe He called me to serve in the church and to encourage and mentor women. Over the years, I have been a counselor and mentor to many at COR. Many young women who have sat under my teaching have gone on to become teachers and leaders themselves in this ministry. It is such a blessing to see that. I am grateful to have helped so many professional women realize, as they climb the corporate ladder, that God has a role in their lives. With God, balance is possible. You never know when you'll need strength beyond what you can imagine, but with God, it is always there.

Losing My Son Raymond to Suicide

On Monday, March 25th, 2013, my ex-husband Ron gave me the call every parent dreads: Our youngest son, Raymond Bernard Scharf II, just twenty-eight years old, had taken his own life.

From the time he was fourteen, Raymond had faced his share of struggles, but we didn't know why. We had taken him to psychologists, unsure of the cause of his unpredictable behavior. At twenty, Raymond was diagnosed with bipolar disorder. In 2013, he was living with Ron in Las Vegas and Ron shared that things had gotten especially tough for him starting in January of that year. We were not entirely sure what triggered the change, but we could tell something was different.

The previous Saturday night around 8 p.m., Raymond had called me. "Mama, I love you so much," he said.

I was caught off guard and responded, "I know that. So, why are you telling me this now? What's going on?"

He quickly replied, "Nothing. I just want you to know how much I love you."

That didn't sit right with me. I asked him again, "Thank you, and you know I love you too. But what's going on? Where are you?" He told me he was at the movies with his dad and that his phone had broken, so he was calling from his dad's phone. I said, "You're at the movies? Are you struggling with something? Don't do anything stupid at the movies."

He laughed and reassured me, "Mama, you know I wouldn't ever hurt anybody. You know me." Then, he added, "Just remember that I love you."

I didn't know what to make of it, so I said, "Ok, but don't hurt yourself either." I'll always remember his response: "Mama, how many times have I told you I would never hurt myself?"

I replied, "You better not."

He said, "I'll call you later. I need to get back in the movies with Dad."

Before we hung up, I reminded him, "Raymond, I have an appointment for you next Thursday with the psychiatrist in Newport Beach. Make sure you're here by Wednesday. It took a lot to get this appointment."

He hesitated and said, "Maybe I'll come."

I told him firmly, "You will come. Be here by Wednesday, okay?"

"Okay," he said. "Just remember that I love you."

I replied, "I know." And that was the last time I ever spoke to my son.

A few weeks earlier, when he had visited, he'd told me he was hearing voices in his head. He said he was unhappy and wanted to stay in the house. I told him I would get him an appointment as soon as I could. He was open to it. As I thought about our conversation, I started to feel really uneasy.

I called Maronya right away and said, "Raymond just called me, and I don't like how I feel. He kept saying he loved me, and he's at the movies with your dad."

She asked, "Is he okay?"

"I don't know," I replied. "He also seemed unsure about coming to the appointment next week."

She said, "He needs to go. I'll call him and encourage him."

My worry was justified. Later that night, around 10:30 p.m., Ron called me.

"Do you know where Raymond is?" he asked. "I saw on my phone that he called you. He drove us to the movies, but now I can't find him, and he's not here to drive us home." I told him about the conversation I had with Raymond earlier, and he said, "I don't know what to think. I'll get a taxi home."

And that was the beginning of the nightmare.

I called Ron back that night and again on Sunday morning, but he still had not heard from Raymond. Something didn't feel right, and I couldn't shake the unease. I went to church that morning and asked for prayers for my son because deep down, I felt like something was wrong. Later, Maronya called the Las Vegas police department and filed a missing person report. After church, Adrian, my oldest son, came over, and we drove around to visit some of Raymond's friends, thinking maybe he'd driven from Las Vegas to California.

Monday morning, I picked up Brenda from John Wayne Airport to head to a meeting in San Diego. Just as we pulled into the meeting location, Ron called me. The moment I heard his voice, I knew something was wrong. My heart started racing, and I began trembling. Then, with a shaky voice, he said, "Martha, they found Raymond's body. He's gone."

I couldn't believe what I heard. My entire body was shaking, and I screamed as I pulled the car into a parking spot. Brenda immediately grabbed my hands, sensing something was terribly wrong. Tears poured down my face as my mind tried to process what Ron had just told me. I kept screaming, "Oh God, oh God!"

Brenda began crying too, softly saying, "Lord, please have mercy," while letting me cry and scream.

Ron said, "I'll call you back. The police are still here with me."

All I could do was cry out, "Oh God, oh God, please, God."

Brenda called Daniel right away and, with a teary voice, told him, "Daniel, you need to come to San Diego to pick up Martha. Ron just called her and told her the police found Raymond, and he's gone." Brenda then stepped out of the car, trying to pull herself together before going into the meeting.

I remained in the car, unable to stop crying. I picked up the phone and called Pastor Mark. Through the tears and screams, I managed to say, "Mark, they found Raymond. He's gone. Help me, Pastor. Please help me." He asked God to comfort me, and he stayed on the phone with me until Daniel arrived. When Daniel got there, I collapsed into his arms. The pain was overwhelming. My heart was shattered, and I couldn't stop crying. All I could do was cling to Daniel as I tried to process the unthinkable.

There are moments in life when you face challenges so overwhelming that nothing else seems to matter. That's exactly where I found myself at that moment. At that point, nothing mattered. Not my dreams, my ambition, my company, my job, my customers, my success, my money, or even my future. It all felt meaningless. My soul felt shattered, and the pain was so intense that for more than three weeks, my bed was the only place I could find even a hint of peace. I couldn't think. I couldn't eat. I couldn't pray. I felt broken, guilty, and completely hopeless. The guilt I felt as a mother was overwhelming. *What could I have done differently? What did I do wrong? What should I have said or done that night?* As a minister, it was even worse. *Why did I not pray with him that night? Why did I not encourage him more? What could I have done, not only as his mother but as a minister?* I couldn't understand what had happened. *What had I done wrong? What did I not do? Why could I not save my son? Why did I not see this coming? Why did he do this? My mind kept spinning with questions. Why, why, why?*

During that time, nothing anyone said could comfort me. No words could ease the pain. The only one who could help me was God. Only God could give me the peace I so desperately needed to repair my broken heart and restore my spirit.

I don't know what challenges, losses, or tragedies you have faced— or might face—but I do know this: When life hits you hard, like my son's death by suicide hit me, you need something greater than yourself. You need a relationship with God, the Almighty, who can give you peace beyond understanding. In John 14:27, Jesus tells the disciples, "Peace I leave with you; my peace I give to you. Do not let your hearts be troubled, and do not be afraid." That peace is what carried me through. Life goes on, even after tragedy, and God is the refuge who gives you the strength to get back up.

Losing my son was the most devastating experience of my life, a pain that words cannot fully articulate. Yet, through this unimaginable heartbreak, I found that leaning on my faith was the only way I could begin to heal and move forward. It taught me that even in the darkest valleys, there is a light that provides comfort and strength. While this testimony is about loss, it's also about the resilience and peace that can be found in trusting God through it all.

Minister Mama Officiated the Weddings

As a minister, I have had the incredible privilege of officiating the weddings of my children: Maronya and Jay, Richard and Shanta, Adrian and Rita, as well as my nephew Pedro and Aisha, and my mentees Terri and Terrance. Each ceremony was a deeply personal and emotional moment, filled with love, joy, and the undeniable presence of God. Standing before them, I felt honored to bless their unions and witness the beginning of such beautiful journeys. It's a humbling experience to play a role in one of the most significant days of someone's life, especially when it's my own family.

These moments were made even more meaningful by the presence of my church community and a few cherished friends, who have also been a significant part of my spiritual journey. Together, we have shared countless milestones, each a reminder of God's grace and guidance in our lives. From the vows exchanged to the prayers shared, these weddings have been a vivid reminder of the power of love, faith, and the enduring blessings that come from trusting in God's plan.

One of the greatest blessings I have received has been baptizing four of my grandchildren: Amari, Kai, Grant, and Aria. The glow in their eyes and the way they smiled as I prayed over them—committing their lives to God and asking for His guidance and protection—brought me so much joy. As part of the legacy I hope to leave, I have made sure that each of my grandchildren has received God's blessing over their lives and a Bible from their Gmama and Grandpa. It is a small yet meaningful gesture, a way to remind them of God's unending love and grace—and of ours—throughout their journey. My hope is that these gifts will serve as a constant source of inspiration and comfort, guiding them as they grow and encounter both the joys and challenges of life.

In 2010, God placed a vision in my heart that completely transformed my understanding of what He was calling me to do. The vision was to create something extraordinary: a spiritual retreat, a restoration center, and a replica of Solomon's temple as the temple of the living God. This vision, which I call ReFresh, is meant to be built on the beautiful island of St. Lucia, a place close to my heart and full of natural beauty that mirrors God's creation in its purest form.

In 2013, I took a leap of faith and wrote down the vision, making it plain, as the Bible instructs in Habakkuk 2:2. I trusted that God would provide, even when this dream felt too big or too far away. Since then, I have witnessed God work in many incredible ways, accomplishing smaller milestones that have brought us closer to this ultimate goal. Each step has strengthened my faith and reminded me that nothing is impossible with God.

ReFresh is more than a project, it's a divine calling to build a space where people can reconnect with God, find restoration, and experience His presence in a powerful way. While the journey has been long, it's also been deeply rewarding, and I trust that God will continue to guide us as we take the next steps toward bringing this vision to fruition. I believe with all my heart that this legacy will honor God and make the world a better place for generations to come.

Lessons in G.U.T.S.

My life has taught me so much, especially that the future is unpredictable. When the unexpected happens, it's only through God's presence that I have found peace. Staying spiritually connected is so important because life will always throw challenges your way, and you'll need God's help to hold onto that peace.

Peace is a priceless gift from God. When you keep Him at the center of your life, that foundation becomes even stronger. His guidance brings clarity in uncertain times, and His love reminds you that you are never alone, no matter how hard things get.

Trusting in God's plan also means surrendering control and believing that He knows what's best for you. It's not always easy, especially when the road ahead seems unclear. Faith requires action. You must choose to trust, even when you cannot see the outcome. Through prayer and reflection, you can align your heart with His will, finding comfort in knowing that His perspective is far greater than yours. With God at the center, even the most challenging seasons can lead to growth, wisdom, and a deeper relationship with Him.

G — Gratitude: I am deeply thankful for the twenty-eight incredible years I had with my son Raymond. Every moment we shared is a treasure that I hold close to my heart. His laughter could light up a room. God has blessed me with the gift of memory, allowing me to revisit those precious moments whenever I need to heal and find solace. Losing Raymond was the most heartbreaking experience of my life, but even in the darkest times, I am grateful for my relationship with God. He has been my rock, offering me the comfort and peace I desperately needed to trust in His plan, even when I didn't understand it. Through prayer, I have found strength, knowing that God sees the bigger picture and works all things for good. No matter what challenges life throws my way, I have faith that I can always turn to Him to guide me with a calm and steady heart, giving me hope and courage to move forward.

U — Unity: Family means everything to me. My relationships with my husband, Daniel, and my children make life so fulfilling and are at the heart of everything I do. Even with a blended family, we have managed to create a peaceful and harmonious dynamic—no "Baby Mama Drama" here—which I know is not always easy to achieve. Daniel and I have worked hard to build a loving and supportive environment for everyone, putting communication and mutual respect at the center of our home. We have faced our share of challenges, but we have always stood together as a united front, no matter the circumstances. It brings me so much joy to see all our children respect and genuinely care for one another, growing up in a space where love and kindness come first. Maintaining that unity hasn't always been simple. It takes effort, patience, and understanding—but those values have helped us build a strong family bond and avoid unnecessary conflict.

T — Trustworthiness: Trustworthiness begins internally and starts with believing in yourself. It's about having confidence in your abilities, knowing you are capable, gifted, and prepared to pursue your dreams, even when the path ahead feels uncertain. When you trust yourself, you lay the foundation for others to trust you too. Success comes from good character, consistent effort, and taking the important first step to believe in your own potential. As you grow to trust God, you develop the strength to face challenges, follow through on commitments, and prove to yourself and others that you are capable of achieving truly great things. Trust is not built overnight, but with every small step forward, you become a person of integrity and determination.

S — Spirituality: There are moments in life when you have to lean on God. For me, one of those moments came during one of the hardest periods of my life when everything felt overwhelming, empty, and hopeless. I didn't know how to move forward or find the strength to keep going after Raymond's death. The only way I got through it was by turning to God with honest, raw conversations. I poured out my heart to Him, sharing my fears, guilt, doubts, and pain. I needed God to restore my soul and give me the peace I could not find anywhere else. It was not immediate, and it did not happen the way I expected. But in His perfect timing, He brought healing and clarity into my life. I know I survived that incredibly difficult time only because of God's grace and unwavering presence.

CHAPTER 16

Don't Let Nobody Turn You Around

*Success is deeply personal, shaped by your dreams, driven by
your determination, and measured by both.*

Several years after IMRI got off the ground and turned a nice
profit, I took my mama with me on a visit to see my employees
at NASA, one of my accounts in Stennis, Mississippi. I had an amazing
team back then. The late Chuck Breath, one of my staff, owned a
beautiful, big boat, and he planned a dinner outing for Mama and me.
She was in her mid-80s at the time.

When we arrived at the boat dock, Chuck and his wife, Ellen, along
with Pete, his wife, Maria, and a few other employees, were there. All
of them were White, and some called me Ms. Daniel, while others just
said Martha. Everyone greeted Mama as Mrs. Holmes, which made
her smile. As we walked toward Chuck's huge white boat, Pete, the
manager, came over to greet us. He opened the car door for my mom
and gave her a big hug.

"Hello, Mrs. Holmes. I'm Pete Furze. I work for Martha here at
NASA. I am so glad you could join us for dinner tonight."

Mama looked a little surprised, but smiled and said, "Hello, and I
am looking forward to it."

Pete walked alongside us on the dock as we approached the boat.

"Mrs. Holmes, do you mind if I help you up on the boat?"

Mama smiled and said, "Certainly, because I don't want to fall down."

Pete chuckled and replied, "There is no way we'd let you do that, ma'am. Let me help you."

As Mama climbed up with Pete's help, his wife, Maria, was waiting at the top of the boat. She reached for Mama's hand to steady her, then walked her over to a big, comfy chair, making sure she was all settled. They treated her like a queen. I followed behind, but stopped to greet the employees, giving hugs and sharing laughs. My sister was with us too, so she politely introduced herself to everyone.

As the evening went on, we mingled with the staff, and I could feel the respect they had for me as the company president. But it was not all formal; there was so much laughter and fun. Everyone made a point to chat with Mama, telling her how much they enjoyed working for me and IMRI. I glanced at Mama a few times, and she was absolutely glowing with all the attention and love. She laughed, smiled, and had the best time.

Chuck walked over to Mama and said, "How do you deal with her? She's always up to something!"

Mama laughed and said, "She came out that way! She was born feet first, and I knew right then she was going to be different." Everyone burst out laughing.

Then, Chuck grinned and said, "You got that right! She's different, but I like her a lot."

Mama looked at me, then back at Chuck, and gave him the sweetest smile.

When it was time for dinner, they brought a small table for Mama, set it up with a tablecloth, and made sure she had everything she needed. All night, they took care of her, and she soaked it all in, happy as could be. When we got back to the dock, they helped Mama off the boat, gave her big hugs, and thanked her for coming. There was so much love and joy that night. The way they treated my mother was incredible.

On the drive back to the hotel, Mama turned to me and said, "Baby, was I really in Mississippi? I cannot believe how all those White folks treated me in Mississippi." She looked at me, started to cry, and said, "I never thought I would live to see so much love and kindness from White people in Mississippi."

She wiped her tears, looked me in the eyes, and said, "Baby, you are somebody. I saw how much they respected you and how they talked about loving working for you." Then she paused and said, "Baby, they said they worked for you! Mama is so proud of you. Girl, you are really somebody big!"

My mother grew up as a sharecropper, in a time and place where Black folks were not allowed to mix with White people. She never imagined seeing a Black person in charge of White people, let alone being their boss. Her entire life, she'd only experienced serving White people, never the other way around.

That moment with my mom reminded me why I do what I do. As a leader and entrepreneur, I want to inspire everyone to chase their dreams. There is so much power inside all of us. If you can dream it, you can live it. And if you live it with passion and determination, you can achieve it. I have faced a lot of challenges, some that felt impossible to overcome. But the truth is, those challenges were not roadblocks, they were steppingstones. They were lessons, opportunities to grow, and reasons to keep pushing forward. No matter how hard things got, I never gave up. I refused to let anyone or anything stop me. Through it all, there was a voice inside me—a spirit I could not ignore—telling me, "Be encouraged. Never give up." And I didn't. Even when the world said "No," that voice inside of me kept shouting "Yes." I let that voice guide me, and I stayed on my path that I defined myself. The beautiful truth is that you can do the same.

Don't let nobody turn you around from your dreams. You have it in you. Keep going and keep believing. If you have a unique vision, your dream deserves to be chased with everything you have. Take a moment to think about the dreams that brought you to where you are today. What is the passion that keeps you going, even when things get tough? Be encouraged and know that you are never walking this path alone. There are people who share your vision and are ready to support you; you just need to be open, grateful, and willing to ask for help. When doubt starts to creep in, lean on those who believe in you. Tap into your network, your mentors, your friends, the people who push you to do better and inspire you to aim higher. Do not let any setback dim your dreams.

As you pursue your goals, visualize yourself as a relentless dreamer, steadfast and unshakeable. Dedicate yourself one hundred percent to making your dream a reality. And develop the G.U.T.S to make it happen. Through it all, never lose sight of your power. You are in control of your success. You are the author of your own story, and success is whatever you decide it is. If you believe you can, you will. If you believe you can't, well, you are probably right.

You've got this. Keep going. Keep dreaming. And keep showing up for yourself. The best is yet to come. Keep striving for the greatness you are capable of. And most importantly, don't ever give up. Like the saying goes: "Don't let nobody turn you around."

About the Author

In 1992, Martha Daniel founded Information Management Resources, Inc. (IMRI) to provide technical consulting services. Under her leadership, IMRI has grown significantly, delivering more than $400+ million in cybersecurity, digital transformation, strategic consulting, and information technology. The company operates in thirteen states and internationally.

IMRI has supported federal, state and local governments, public and commercial clients including the Executive Office of the President; U.S. Congressional Budget Office; Defense Information Systems Agency (DISA); U.S. Navy; U.S. Army; Department of Homeland Security (DHS); Office of the Undersecretary of Defense (DOD); National Aeronautics and Space Administration (NASA); the U.S. Intelligence Community, and numerous Fortune 500 companies. IMRI is noted as a highly skilled, results-oriented organization, and is also distinguished by its status as a service-disabled veteran (U.S. Navy), woman-owned, small, disadvantaged business.

After twelve years of intense cybersecurity experience, Martha co-founded Cytellix Corporation, a cybersecurity company, to develop an artificial intelligence (AI) platform of governance and risk management services targeting Cybersecurity Regulatory Compliance and Risk Management solutions and services as a Managed Security Services Provider (MSSP). Cytellix provides a comprehensive suite of cyber security solutions that identify, control, and audit critical cyber assets enabling clients to reduce infrastructure and operational risks, and improve their organization's cybersecurity compliance, threat and risk postures.

A published author and frequent speaker, Martha has previously co-authored two books: *On the Other Side of Midnight 2000: An Executive Guide to the Year 2000 Problem* and *Million Dollar Conversations*. She was featured in the book *Women in Security* by Debra Christofferson.

In 2010 she participated as a study group member for the Presidential National Infrastructure Advisory Council's (NIAC) Water Sector Resilience Final Report and Recommendations. She has been quoted as an industry spokesperson for a variety of publications and was honored by the White House in 2014 under President Barack Obama as one of "10 Women Veteran Champions of Change." Other notable awards include the 2020 Orange County Business Journal Family-Owned Business Award; 2020 and 2019 Top Woman Owned Business in Orange County; 2018 Top 100 Most Influential People in Orange County; 2018 Hall of Fame Induction for African American-Owned Businesses by City National Bank and Hart Foundation; and the 2016 and 2000 SBA Small Business of the Year. In addition, IMRI/Cytellix have received numerous technology innovation awards including the 2018, 2019, and 2020 Stevie Award for most innovative cybersecurity technology.

Martha graduated with honors, earning her bachelor's degree in computer information systems from California State Polytechnic University, Pomona and her master's degree in business administration from the University of La Verne. She is an ordained minister at Christ Our Redeemer African Methodist Episcopal Church in Irvine, California, a Board Trustee with the University of La Verne, former Chairperson of the Board Development Committee of Orange County United Way, and a member of the Trusteeship of the Los Angeles Chapter of International Women's Forum (IWF).

She lives in Temecula, California with her husband, Mathurin (Daniel). Together, they have a blended family of nine children (one deceased) and are proud grandparents to fourteen grandchildren.

Memorable Reflections

*R*eflecting on all of the memorable experiences that have left a lasting mark on my journey to achieve my dreams, I realize that while others have influenced and supported me with advice, encouragement, and guidance, I have always made sure to take charge of my own destiny. That said, I must give credit to the grace of God. He has been the steady hand guiding me through challenges, setbacks, and successes. From prayers and education to career opportunities, mentors, friends, family, and even travel, God's wisdom has been the key to it all.

I am filled with gratitude for some special people and experiences that have shaped my journey:

1. **A supportive and loving husband:** My husband, Mathurin Daniel, has been my rock. He has sacrificed so much, even quitting his own jobs at times to help me in nearly every position within our company. Over the past thirty-three years, he has given me wisdom, encouragement, and unwavering support. He dried my tears during tough times and celebrated with me during the good ones. In fact, it was his idea for me to write this book. His belief in me has been incredible. Special thanks to Debi Larrison, my close friend in New York, and Daniel for encouraging me to bring his vision for this project to life.

2. **Raising and influencing a legacy:** I am proud to say I have successfully raised and influenced the lives of nine children:

Adrian, Maronya, Raymond (Deceased), Stephanie, Bradley, Shanta, Natalie, Eliezar, and Lizar. In addition, I have built a legacy for my fourteen grandchildren: Isaiah, Jordan, Zion, Grant, Jaden, Amari, Kai, Aria, Ava, Mya, William, Jade, Ajahnai, and Jasmine. They all love and respect me, which is the greatest gift I could ever ask for.

3. **Passing down a family business:** One of my proudest moments has been passing down our second-generation family business to my amazing daughter, Maronya Moultrie. She joined me on this journey in 2009, and since then, we have built a successful business and an incredible bond. We have traveled the world together. I know she's dedicated to keeping our values alive and making sure our story is passed on to the next generation. My daughter is my everything: smart, a wonderful mom, an outstanding attorney, a great wife, and a strong leader. I could not be more proud of her. This apple did not fall far from the tree!

4. **My business partner and close friend:** For more than twenty-four years, I have had the absolute privilege of working alongside one of the smartest women I know, Brenda Taylor. She has been more than just a business partner; she is a close friend and truly like a sister to me. Brenda has been loyal, dedicated, and an incredible part of my journey in business and chasing my dreams. If there is anyone who has my utmost respect, it's Brenda. She just gets me. She knows exactly how to handle my personality. She's also deeply rooted in her faith, and over the years, we have prayed together, cried together, encouraged each other, and celebrated success side by side. Brenda has given me her all, and together we have grown in so many ways: spiritually, financially, intellectually, and professionally. I am truly blessed to have her in my life.

5. **My best friend:** Sandra Floyd is like my sister from another mother. We have been friends for more than thirty years, and she's always had my back in business and in life. She runs her own staffing company, and we talk almost every day, sharing advice, encouragement, and plenty of laughs. Sandra has loving, nurturing energy, and I am grateful to have her in my life. Her husband Kit and their adorable fur baby, Hershey (my little doggy nephew) have shared so many great moments with us, both in the Bay Area and when they visit our home. They are truly family.

6. **My spiritual sister:** Bonita Dent is like my other sister, thanks to Mama Pauletta Houston. Her husband, Von, and Daniel have definitely had their hands full dealing with the two of us! We have traveled to many countries together and taken countless road trips. For almost twenty years now, we have shared a close friendship. Bonita has been there for me through my entire ministry journey, always cheering me on and celebrating the big moments. When she is in the room, you can guarantee there is going to be laughter.

7. **Making It Real Women Bible Study (WBS):** Leading the Bible study at Christ Our Redeemer AME Church (COR) since 2004 has been one of the most rewarding parts of my spiritual journey. Mentoring Terri Kelly-Jones, President of WBS, has been a joy both spiritually and professionally. I'm confident Terri will carry this ministry's legacy forward for many years after my transition from this earth. For twenty-one years, we have hosted an annual women's retreat—bringing women together to fellowship, grow spiritually, and embrace the Lord on cruise ships, weekend resort getaways, and special gatherings at my home. This ministry has deepened my faith and, by God's grace, has blessed many women as they continue to grow in their own spiritual walks.

I am overwhelmed with gratitude for every person, every experience, and every opportunity that has brought me here. This journey has been nothing short of incredible, and I thank God every day for the blessings He has given me.

I am deeply grateful to everyone who played a role in this book's journey. To my incredible beta readers, thank you for your time, insights, and honest feedback that helped shape this story into its best form. Dr. Jarvis Pahl, Bonita Dent, Maronya Moultrie, Aisha Daniel, Deborah Larrison, Betty LaMarr, and Dr. Mable Springfield Scott, your perspectives were invaluable, and your support meant the world to me.

A heartfelt thank you also goes to those who participated in the selection of my book cover. Mathurin Daniel, Bonita Dent, Sandra O. Floyd, Brian Brick, Pedro Daniel, Gaynelle Hendricks, Hoshi Printer, Deborah Larrison, Dr. Jarvis Pahl, Betty LaMarr, Doniel Sutton, Ruth Ko, Andre Julian, Brenda Taylor, Aisha Brent, Ed Hart, Ken Ashford, Dr. Mable Springfield Scott, and Brian Berger. Your input and enthusiasm brought this vision to life. I am forever thankful for your contributions to this creative endeavor.

Author Coach: I want to express my upmost sincere gratitude to Anita R. Henderson, CEO and Founder of Write Your Life, also known as "The Author's Midwife." Your guidance, as my author coach, was invaluable in shaping the narrative and ensuring the content reached the highest level of professional excellence. Your team's expertise was instrumental in navigating the intricate process of manuscript development.

Publisher: I also wish to extend my thanks to Melanie Johnson and Jenn Foster of Elite Online Publishing. Your leadership as publishing strategists in the digital publishing space provided a strong foundation to achieve my goals for the success of this book.